The Homeowner's Guide to Surface Preparation for Interior House Painting

The Step-by-Step Guide to Preparing Surfaces for:

Paint

Decorative Paint

Faux Finish

Stencils

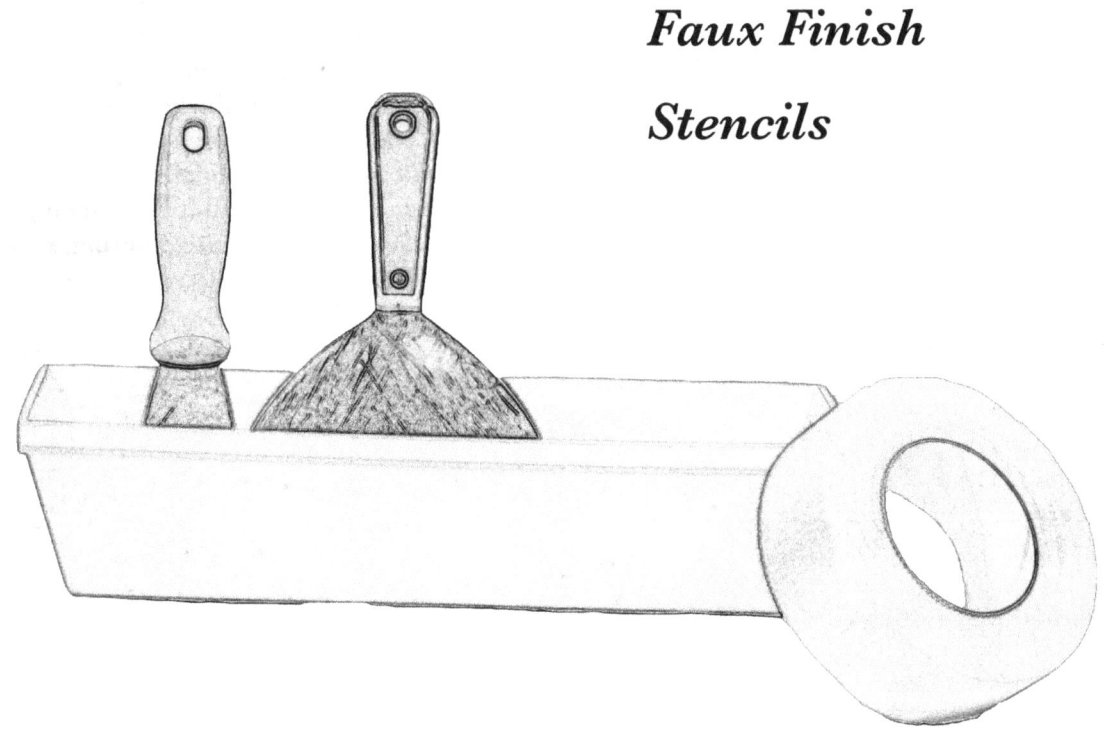

Steve Broujos

The Homeowner's Guide to Surface Preparation for Interior House Painting

Copyright © 2011 by Steve Broujos

FIRST EDITION

All rights reserved. No part of this book may be copied, reproduced, scanned, downloaded, transmitted, broadcast or distributed in any form or by any means electronic or mechanical without written permission from the Author.

Disclaimer

The information provided in this book should not be considered as a replacement for the professional services of a house painting contractor, carpenter, drywall contractor, plasterer or other skilled tradesman. Nor should the information provided in this book be used as a replacement for any direction for use or safety precaution that is listed or provided by the manufacturer of any tool, material or supply that is used when preparing, repairing or painting interior surfaces. Always read and follow the manufacturer's directions for use and safety precautions. Understand all directions for use and safety precautions before beginning surface preparation, repair and painting work. Understand the information provided in this book before beginning surface preparation work. Any endeavor involving labor, material and tool use involves some measure of risk and the potential of personal injury, injury to others (which may include family members and pets), damage to property, loss and unsatisfactory results. Always work in a safe, sober, informed and controlled manner, as failure to do so can result in personal injury, injury to others, damage to property, loss and unsatisfactory results. The use of tools used in surface preparation, home repair and house painting can cause Carpal Tunnel Syndrome and other repetitive use injuries. It is the responsibility of the individual or individuals undertaking the surface preparation, repair and painting of their home to protect themselves, their family, their pets and those entering their home from the hazards they may encounter as a result of performing, or being in the vicinity of, surface preparation, repair and painting work. This book has been carefully written to provide information that is as accurate, complete and reliable as is possible. As personal skill and conditions present on each surface preparation and painting project will vary, no warranty of results can be made or is implied regarding the use of the information provided in this book. If you are not absolutely certain of your ability to safely and properly complete any surface preparation technique, repair or task covered in this book, hire a licensed professional. Anyone renovating, repairing or preparing interior surfaces should stay informed as to changes in product technology, safety procedures and Federal and local law that affect surface preparation, interior house painting, renovation and home repair. Obtain any needed permits for home repairs. Referenced resources may change at any time. The Author and publisher of this book will not be held responsible or liable for any personal injury, injury to others, damage, loss, or unsatisfactory results which are deemed to have occurred directly or indirectly from the use of the information provided in this book.

Steve Broujos LLC
P. O. Box 126
Montchanin DE 19710-0126

www.LearnHousePainting.com

Illustrations and Cover Design by
Matthew Schroeder
Double-edged Design
double-edged.com

Manufactured in the United States of America

Fortune favors the brave. Drive on is my motto.
James Eads

Table of Contents

	PAGE

SECTION 1   PREPARING FOR SURFACE PREPARATION

CHAPTER 1   SAFETY — 15

Before surface preparation begins	16
When preparing surfaces, protect eyes, respiratory system, ears and hands	20
Guidelines for safely using tools, materials and supplies	22
Protecting children	23
Protecting pets	23
Avoiding spontaneous combustion fire	24
Turn off electric power to the work area	25

CHAPTER 2   INTRODUCTION TO MATERIALS AND SUPPLIES — 27

Materials	28
Supplies	32
Masking tapes used in surface preparation and painting	33

CHAPTER 3   TASKS TO COMPLETE BEFORE SURFACE PREPARATION BEGINS — 37

Locate and repair water leaks	43
Repair water-damaged surfaces	43
Replace damaged wood trim	43
Remove wallpaper and borders	44
Clean wallpaper and border paste residue	45, 49
Clean soiled surfaces	45
Clean mildewed surfaces	46
Remove mold from surfaces	47
Have a plasterer inspect plaster surfaces and repair plaster surface damage	47
Hire a drywall contractor to replace damaged drywall	48

CHAPTER 4   WORKPLACE LIGHTING — 51

Work lights	52

Section II Surface Preparation Techniques and Repairs

Chapter 5 Surface Preparation Techniques — 57

- Using a 6" taping knife to apply repair compounds — 60
  - Tips for skillful taping knife use — 62
- Application of drywall joint compound — 64
- Application of lightweight spackling compound — 68
- Application of spackling compound — 72
- Skim coating — 76
  - Skim coating ceiling and wall surfaces with drywall joint compound — 77
  - Skim coating wood trim surfaces with spackling compound — 82
- Using painter's putty to fill nail sets and miter gaps on wood surfaces — 85
- Sanding — 88
  - Sanding tools — 90
  - Dustless sanding — 92
- Caulking — 95
- Priming and sealing — 100
  - Priming and sealing situations — 101
  - Spot priming and full coat priming — 104

Chapter 6 Common Surface Preparation Repairs — 107

- Concealing non-flush repairs by applying joint compound with correct shape and contour — 110
- How to sand non-flush surface preparation repairs — 113
- Repairing holes and damaged areas with a wall repair patch — 115
- Repairing holes and indentations in wood surfaces with wood filler — 120
- Repairing drywall nail pops — 124
- Repair of surfaces with plastic anchors and metal Molly bolt jackets — 131
- Supporting cracked ceiling drywall and refastening sagging ceiling drywall — 134
- Repairing cracks — 140
  - Repairing cracks with self-adhesive mesh drywall joint tape and drywall joint compound — 144
- Tips for working with self-adhesive mesh drywall joint tape — 149
- Repairing drywall cover damage — 152

Chapter 7 Repairing Surface Defects — 159

- Surface grit — 162
- Air bubble holes in applied drywall joint compound — 164
- Inadequate drywall joint compound application over drywall joint tape — 166
- Lifting or bubbling (blistering) of drywall joint tape — 168
- Inadequate sanding of drywall joint compound — 171
- Inadequate wet sanding of drywall joint compound — 173
- Raised drywall cover damage caused by sanding — 176
- Protruding drywall screw heads — 178

SECTION III APPENDICES AND INDEX

APPENDIX 1	REFERENCE OF SURFACE PREPARATION TECHNIQUES AND REPAIRS	184
APPENDIX 2	REFERENCE OF SURFACE PREP TIP BOXES	185

INDEX   187

Foreword

Surface preparation is the most important part of every interior house painting project. Whether you are applying paint, decorative paint, faux finish or stencils, the quality of your surface preparation directly affects the appearance and durability of every painted surface.

Surface preparation may also be viewed as a valuable decorating tool, as surface preparation craftsmanship leads to painted surfaces that are quickly noticed and often praised. Paint provides color, but attention to surface preparation detail helps to make the interior of your home look truly exceptional.

The Homeowner's Guide to Surface Preparation for Interior House Painting is the updated, revised and renamed version of its predecessor, *Surface Preparation for Interior House Painting*. (2007)

Important updates and revisions include:

- **The Environmental Protection Agency's (EPA) Renovate, Repair and Painting Rule (RRP)**
  Safety information concerning the prevention of lead hazards when renovating, repairing and house painting, is available from the EPA at **www.epa.gov/lead/pubs/renovation.htm**. Protect yourself and your family before beginning surface preparation by reading the information provided for homeowners on the EPA's website at the link provided above.
  (More about the RRP Rule and the EPA's information for homeowners can be found on Page 16)

- **A significant increase in the number of cross-references**
  The cross-references provided throughout the text will help you to quickly access needed information. They also provide a bridge to related areas of the text for greater understanding of the technique, repair or task you are working on. The cross-references also serve to reinforce learning.

- **A larger section with more information covering crack repair with self-adhesive mesh drywall joint tape and drywall joint compound**

The Homeowner's Guide to Surface Preparation for Interior House Painting has been carefully written to help you prepare interior surfaces correctly- the first time. Correct surface preparation helps to save you time, money and considerable aggravation. It also helps you to achieve results of which you can be proud.

My step-by-step interior surface preparation technique and repair methods were originally developed for the instruction of decorative painters and muralists, who need the highest level of surface preparation possible for commissioned decorative finishes and murals.

Great success in surface preparation.

Steve

How to Use This Book

READ THE TEXT COMPLETELY BEFORE BEGINNING SURFACE PREPARATION

A complete reading of the text is helpful to familiarize the reader with the process of interior surface preparation. Each chapter builds a base of reference needed for clear understanding of the instruction presented in later chapters. Chapters 1-4 present information and provide tasks to complete to prepare the reader and the house for surface preparation. Chapters 5-7 cover the surface preparation techniques and repairs used when preparing interior surfaces. The Appendices provide reference information pertaining to the surface preparation techniques, repairs and tips, covered in this book. Reading the text with a family member or friend can help to increase learning!

REFER TO CHAPTER 1 AND THE AMBULANCE BOXES FOR SAFETY INFORMATION

Chapter 1 has been written to be a resource of safety information. Read, learn and follow the instruction provided for working safely. The website addresses listed in the chapter will lead you to important safety information. The phone numbers provided will put you in contact with government agencies should you have questions or concerns.

The Homeowner's Guide to Surface Preparation for Interior House Painting **emphasizes working safely. Important safety information can be found where you see the ambulance symbol.**

REFER TO THE Surface Prep Tip BOXES FOR HELPFUL TIPS

Surface Prep Tip

Surface Prep Tip boxes

The Surface Prep Tip boxes located throughout the text provide useful information to improve your surface preparation skill.

How to Use This Book

REFER TO THE *Estimated Time to Complete* BOXES FOR AN APPROXIMATE START-TO-FINISH TIME AND ACTUAL WORKING TIME FOR EACH TECHNIQUE AND REPAIR

Estimated Time to Complete

Estimated Time to Complete boxes are provided after each surface preparation technique and repair. They give you an approximate start-to-finish time and an approximate actual working time for the technique or repair.

REFER TO THE TIPS AND TROUBLESHOOTING BOXES FOR MORE INFORMATION ABOUT THE FINER POINTS OF THE TASK

TIPS AND TROUBLESHOOTING

TIPS AND TROUBLESHOOTING boxes are also provided after each surface preparation technique and repair. They give you more information about the finer points of the task. The answers to the questions that you may have while completing the technique or repair will often be found in the **TIPS AND TROUBLESHOOTING** box. A careful review of the text should answer any remaining questions.

PRACTICE THE SURFACE PREPARATION TECHNIQUES AND REPAIRS

Practice the surface preparation techniques and repairs in rooms such as the garage, laundry room or in closets. These rooms can provide good places to learn before working in the more prominent rooms of your home. Practice until you see good results and feel confident in your ability.

If your home lacks a garage or other room where you can practice, then purchase drywall and small pieces of wood from the local home center. A full sheet of either ³/₈" or ¹/₂" drywall can be cut into two-foot widths to make four practice boards that are two-feet by four-feet. These pieces of cut drywall are used in my surface preparation classes to demonstrate and practice many of the surface preparation techniques and repairs presented in this book. Shelf wood and pieces of wood trim can be hit lightly with a hammer and drilled with holes to create practice surfaces to learn the wood filling and wood skim coating repairs. The local home center may have damaged drywall and scrap wood that can be purchased at reduced cost.

Section 1

Preparing for Surface Preparation

Safety

Chapter 1 is a resource of safety information. Read, learn and follow the instruction provided for working safely. The website addresses listed in the chapter will lead you to important safety information. The phone numbers provided will put you in contact with government agencies should you have questions or concerns. Research, study and stay informed of the important topics covered in this chapter.

Protect your safety, and the safety and well-being of your family. Prepare to work safely before surface preparation begins.

Always work safely.

Note: It is possible that the online resources referenced in this chapter may change at any time.

BEFORE SURFACE PREPARATION BEGINS

1. *See your doctor*

   Surface preparation involves physical exertion and exposure to dust that may be harmful to breathe. Dust created during surface preparation may also irritate the respiratory system and eyes. Individuals with heart, respiratory system or eye problems, and those who are not conditioned for or unaccustomed to physical labor, should obtain clearance from their doctor or physician before beginning surface preparation work.

   NO surface preparation or painting work should be done in a home where a woman is pregnant, or is anticipating becoming pregnant.

2. *Be informed as to the hazards of lead*

   Homes and buildings constructed before 1978 may have the presence of lead-based paint. If your home was built before 1978, be informed as to the hazards of lead.

THE EPA'S RENOVATE, REPAIR AND PAINTING RULE (RRP)

The goal of the EPA's Renovate, Repair and Painting Rule (RRP) is to prevent lead dust hazards that can result from renovation, repair and painting work that is done on homes and buildings built before 1978. If your home was built before 1978, go to the EPA's website listed below and click on the link "Information for Homeowners Working at Home." Read the information provided **before** beginning surface preparation work.

Important information for homeowners can be found at:

www.epa.gov/lead/pubs/renovation.htm

Click on the link "Information for Homeowners Working at Home"

ADDITIONAL INFORMATION ABOUT LEAD

> For more information about lead, contact the National Lead Information Center. Phone: 1-800-424-5323 or log on to: www.epa.gov/lead
>
> An article on the topic of lead-based paint is available from the Consumer Products Safety Commission. CPSC Document #5055 titled "CPSC Warns About Hazards of "Do It Yourself" Removal of Lead Based Paint: Safety Alert." This document can be found on the Internet at the following address:
>
> www.cpsc.gov/cpscpub/pubs/5055.html

3. *Remove mold*

Cleaning, preparing or repairing, mold-damaged or mold-affected surfaces may cause the spread of mold spores in your home. Breathing mold spores can cause sickness. If you have (or suspect that you may have) mold-damaged or mold-affected surfaces in your home, consult a licensed professional mold remediation contractor.

> For more information about mold, log on to the Centers for Disease Control and Prevention (CDC) website: www.cdc.gov. In the search box, type the word "mold."

4. *Address asbestos concerns*

In older homes and structures, asbestos can be found in some construction materials that affect surface preparation for interior house painting. These materials may include ceiling texturing materials, drywall joint compound (also called "wallboard compound"), wood filler, spackling compound, caulk and insulation. The removal of asbestos from construction materials began to gain momentum in the 1970's.

Note: Materials other than those listed above may also contain asbestos.

Why asbestos-containing materials can pose a hazard

Asbestos-containing materials can pose a hazard should asbestos fibers become airborne. Asbestos fibers can become airborne when asbestos-containing materials are scored, sawed, cut, crushed, broken, drilled, scraped, sanded or disturbed. Once airborne, asbestos fibers that are breathed into the lungs can cause health problems, including lung cancer, and other cancers.

When preparing surfaces

If you are unsure of the possibility of asbestos content in any material within the work area, contact a qualified environmental services company. A sample of the material in question should be tested before surface preparation work begins. Testing will determine if asbestos is present. Follow local asbestos removal laws should asbestos be found.

Additional sources of information

Good sources of information about asbestos include government agencies. The box below lists two government agency websites which provide asbestos information. The box at the bottom of *Page 21* has an OSHA web page that also provides asbestos information.

For more information about asbestos log onto:

www.epa.gov/asbestos

www.cdc.gov/niosh/topics/asbestos

For information about asbestos laws in your area, contact your state and local government offices.

---

5. *Visit a Workplace Safety Equipment store*

Workplace Safety Equipment stores have the equipment that you will need for working safely. There you will find equipment to protect your eyes, respiratory system, ears and hands.

Respiratory system protection

It is important to discuss respiratory system protection with a trained professional. Based on the age or your house, the materials that you will be working with and around, and the surface preparation, repair and painting tasks that you need to complete, a respiratory system protection professional will be able to provide the protective equipment and instruction for use that you need to work safely.

Write down and use the recommended respiratory system protection equipment for each surface preparation technique, repair and painting task. As some surface preparation technique and repair steps may require different respiratory system protection equipment, be sure to wear the correct respiratory system protection for each step.

For maximum respiratory system protection, have a trained professional fit and seal-check any respiratory system protection mask that uses replaceable filters. As respiratory system protection masks that use replaceable filters are effective when custom fitted and seal-checked for only one user, each person working on the surface preparation and painting project will need to have their own fitted and seal-checked mask.

When a replaceable filter mask is needed, be sure to have the correct filters installed to protect yourself against the dust particles and/or organic vapors (chemical solvent fumes) for which you will be exposed. Replace filters as directed by the manufacturer's instructions.

Note for men:
Be sure to shave before going to the Workplace Safety Equipment store. Replaceable filter respiratory system protection masks can only be properly fitted and seal-checked to a clean-shaven face.

For additional information, be sure to read *Respiratory system protection, on Page 20.*

*Footnote*_____

Some information used in this section was found on the websites whose addresses appear on Pages 16-18.

When preparing surfaces, protect eyes, respiratory system, ears and hands

1. *Eye protection*

   Eye protection should be worn whenever you are cleaning, preparing, repairing or painting interior surfaces. It should also be worn when setting up and cleaning up the work area.

   > **Sources of information about eye protection**
   >
   > Companies that manufacture and companies that sell workplace safety equipment.
   >
   > The Occupational Safety and Health Administration (OSHA)
   > Phone: 1-800-321-6742 or log on to: www.osha.gov

2. *Respiratory system protection*

   Respiratory system protection should be worn whenever surface preparation or repair results in the creation of dust, such as when sanding surfaces. Dust may also be created when surfaces or materials are scraped, cut or disturbed. Wear respiratory system protection whenever you are in a dusty work area.

   Wear respiratory system protection whenever the fumes of a solvent-based material are present, or will be present, in the work area. Respiratory system protection should be worn whenever you are applying an oil-based primer, primer/sealer, undercoater or paint. It should also be worn when applying White-Pigmented Shellac. Respiratory system protection should be worn whenever you are using paint thinner, mineral spirits, denatured alcohol, paint deglosser, or any other chemical solvent-based product used in surface preparation, interior house painting, or home decorating.

   Respiratory system protection should also be worn whenever you are setting up or cleaning up the work area.

   Wear respiratory system protection when directed to do so by the manufacturer's instructions for any tool, material or supply that you use when cleaning, preparing, repairing or painting interior surfaces. Wear the respiratory system protection equipment recommended by the manufacturer.
   (For more information see Page 19, Visit a Workplace Safety Equipment store)

   > **Sources of information about respiratory system protection**
   >
   > Companies that manufacture and companies that sell workplace safety equipment.
   >
   > The National Institute of Occupational Safety and Health (NIOSH)
   > Phone: 1-412-386-4000 or log on to: www.cdc.gov/niosh/homepage.html.

3. *Ear and hearing protection*

   Ear and hearing protection can help to protect your ears and hearing when using power tools.

   > **SOURCES OF INFORMATION ABOUT EAR AND HEARING PROTECTION**
   >
   > Companies that manufacture and companies that sell workplace safety equipment.
   >
   > The Occupational Safety and Health Administration (OSHA)
   > Phone: 1-800-321-6742 or log on to: www.osha.gov

4. *Hand protection*

   There are many instances where work gloves can and should be worn to protect hands during surface preparation. Light work gloves can be worn to protect hands when sanding surfaces. They can also be worn to protect hands during tool use. Wear work gloves when cleaning up the work area. Wear chemical-resistant rubber work gloves when washing surfaces with a Tri-Sodium Phosphate cleaner, often referred to as "TSP." *(See Page 34)* Wear chemical-resistant rubber work gloves when removing wallpaper paste residue with a wallpaper paste removing product. *(See Pages 45 and 49)* Wear chemical-resistant rubber work gloves when applying a paint deglosser, or when using a paint removing product.

   Wear work gloves when directed to do so by the manufacturer's instructions for any tool, material or supply that you use when cleaning, preparing, repairing or painting interior surfaces. Wear the type of work gloves recommended by the manufacturer.

   > **SOURCES OF INFORMATION ABOUT HAND PROTECTION**
   >
   > Companies that manufacture and companies that sell workplace safety equipment.
   >
   > The Occupational Safety and Health Administration (OSHA)
   > Phone: 1-800-321-6742 or log on to: www.osha.gov

5. *Additional safety information*

   > **ADDITIONAL INFORMATION ON SAFETY AND HEALTH TOPICS IS AVAILABLE BY LOGGING ON TO:**
   >
   > www.osha.gov/SLTC/   Note: SLTC is case sensitive.
   > Phone: 1-800-321-6742

GUIDELINES FOR SAFELY USING TOOLS, MATERIALS AND SUPPLIES

1. Read and follow the directions for use and safety precautions of all tools, materials and supplies used when cleaning, preparing and repairing surfaces for interior house painting. Contact the manufacturer whenever you are unclear about any direction for use or safety precaution. **DO NOT** use any tool, material or supply until you fully understand all directions for use and safety precautions.

2. Always work in a safe, sober, informed and controlled manner. **DO NOT** consume alcoholic beverages before, or during, the time of use of any tool, material or supply used when cleaning, preparing or repairing of interior surfaces. If frustrated or angered, refrain from using any tool, material or supply used in the cleaning, preparing or repairing of interior surfaces. **DO NOT** begin or continue working until you are able to work in a controlled manner.

3. Putty knives, taping knives, scrapers, utility knives and other tools used when preparing and repairing interior surfaces have metal edges, sharp blades and moving parts that can inflict cuts and cause injury during use. Always work carefully with tools.

4. Inspect electric tools before use. Check electric power tool cords and plugs for fraying and damage. A frayed cord or damaged plug can cause electric shock. Before beginning surface preparation work, have any frayed cords or damaged plugs repaired, or replace the electric tool.

5. Have a fresh blade in your utility knife when cutting the nozzle on a tube of caulk.

6. **DO NOT** leave lit or hot work lights unattended.

7. Use caution and care when working and walking on covered (protected for work) flooring surfaces.

Surface Prep Tip

Two-Drop Rule

A wise contractor taught me the Two-Drop Rule when working with tools. Should you drop a tool for the second time, you are too tired to work safely. Take a break, or continue your work the following day. This is good advice, as fatigue can lead to injury. Be safe, DO NOT prepare or repair interior surfaces when fatigued.

Protecting children

1. Keep surface preparation tools, materials and supplies out of the reach of children.

2. Children should be kept away from the work area at all times. Dust generated by surface preparation and repair can be harmful for children to breathe.

3. Always set a good example for children by working safely and teaching safe working habits.

Protecting pets

1. Keep surface preparation tools, materials and supplies out of the reach of pets.

2. Pets should be kept away from the work area at all times. Dust generated by surface preparation and repair can be harmful for pets to breathe.

AVOIDING SPONTANEOUS COMBUSTION FIRE

A spontaneous combustion fire can be caused by an accumulation of flammable vapors (fumes). These vapors can be ignited when exposed to flame, a spark or heat. In some instances, the heat generated by the vapors themselves can cause ignition, resulting in fire. Solvent-based painting materials and supplies such as oil-based primer, oil-based primer/sealer, oil-based paint, White-Pigmented Shellac, paint deglosser, paint thinner, turpentine, mineral spirits and denatured alcohol emit flammable vapors.

To help prevent a spontaneous combustion fire, read and follow the safety precautions listed on the container of each solvent-based material and supply that you use during interior surface preparation and house painting. **Pay close attention to safety warnings and safety instructions concerning proper ventilation and the prevention of flammable vapor (fume) ignition.**

DO NOT ball up, pile, stack or fold any wiping cloth, rag, towel, drop cloth or piece of work clothing that becomes moistened or wet due to contact with a solvent-based primer, primer/sealer, White-Pigmented Shellac, paint deglosser, paint, painting material, painting supply or other solvent-based material or supply. The flammable vapors (fumes) concentrated in any of the above balled up, piled, stacked or folded items can generate enough heat to cause a spontaneous combustion fire.

Before folding, storing or discarding a drop cloth, or any other protective covering, allow any material on the drop cloth or protective covering to fully dry.

Solvent-moistened, or wet, wiping cloths, rags, towels, drop cloths, protective coverings, and work clothes, should be immersed in water and allowed to fully air dry outdoors in an opened position that provides for good airflow.

To safely prepare solvent-moistened, or wet, wiping cloths, rags, and towels for disposal, place them in a metal, water-filled can and seal with a lid. Empty metal cans with lids can be purchased at your local paint store or home center. For disposal information, contact you local Solid Waste Authority. *(Also see Surface Prep Tip: Disposing of primers, paints, materials and supplies, at the bottom of Page 31)*

Contact your local Solid Waste Authority should you have questions concerning the safe disposal of anything pertaining to surface preparation, house painting, or home repair.

Turn off electric power to the work area

Turn off electric power to the work area at the breaker box or fuse box before work begins. Use a heavy-gauge extension cord, or cords, to bring power to the work area for your halogen work light and electric tools.

Should damage occur to a switch, outlet, wire or electrical fixture during surface preparation, contact a licensed professional electrician immediately. Electric power should remain off, or be turned off, in the work area until turned on by the electrician.

Introduction to Materials and Supplies

This chapter provides basic information about common materials and supplies needed for preparing interior surfaces. After describing your surface preparation project, a knowledgeable salesperson at your local paint store or home center can provide the materials and supplies that you will need. If you also need a few surface preparation tools, you will be able to purchase them there as well.

For best results, always purchase and use the highest quality surface preparation and painting tools, materials and supplies.

Materials

Drywall Joint Compound

Drywall joint compound, also called "joint compound" or "mud," can be used to fill small holes and indentations in both drywall and plaster surfaces. More uses of joint compound include crack repair and skim coating. Joint compound is not recommended for repairs to wood surfaces.

(See APPLICATION OF DRYWALL JOINT COMPOUND, on Page 64)

Plaster application: Apply joint compound only to the white coat layer of plaster. (which includes primer/sealer and paint already applied to the white coat layer) Joint compound will not adhere durably to plaster brown coat, lath boards, lath rock or wire screen.

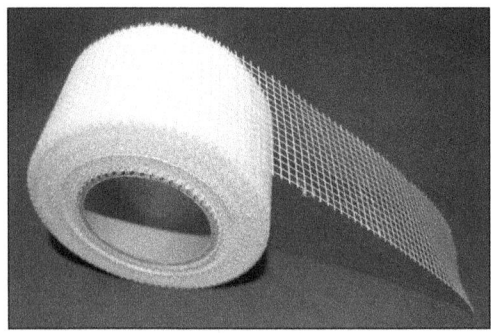

Self-Adhesive Mesh Drywall Joint Tape

Self-adhesive mesh drywall joint tape, also called "mesh tape," can be used to cover the joints of replacement pieces, or full sheets, of drywall. It is also used to cover cracks during crack repair with joint compound. During the repair of drywall cover damage, mesh tape can be used to secure and protect torn edge and brown paper layer damage. Mesh tape has an adhesive side that fastens securely to both drywall and plaster surfaces.

(See Self-adhesive mesh drywall joint tape, on Page 143)

(See REPAIRING CRACKS WITH SELF-ADHESIVE MESH DRYWALL JOINT TAPE AND DRYWALL JOINT COMPOUND, on Page 144)

(See TIPS FOR WORKING WITH SELF-ADHESIVE MESH DRYWALL JOINT TAPE, on Page 149)

(See REPAIRING DRYWALL COVER DAMAGE, on Page 152)

Plaster application: Apply mesh tape only to the white coat layer of plaster (which includes primer/sealer and paint already applied to the white coat layer). Mesh tape will not adhere durably to plaster brown coat, lath boards, lath rock or wire screen.

Lightweight Spackling Compound

Lightweight spackling compound has a light texture which resists sagging. It can be used to fill holes and indentations in drywall, plaster and wood surfaces.

(See APPLICATION OF LIGHTWEIGHT SPACKLING COMPOUND, *on Page 68)*

Plaster application: Apply lightweight spackling compound only to the white coat layer of plaster. (which includes primer/sealer and paint already applied to the white coat layer) Lightweight spackling compound will not adhere durably to plaster brown coat, lath boards, lath rock or wire screen.

Spackling Compound

Spackling compound is a paste-like material that can be used to fill holes and indentations in drywall, plaster and wood surfaces. It has a hard, durable finish making it ideal for skim coating wood surfaces, such as windowsills.

(See APPLICATION OF SPACKLING COMPOUND, *on Page 72)*

(See SKIM COATING WOOD TRIM SURFACES WITH SPACKLING COMPOUND, *on Page 82)*

Plaster application: Apply spackling compound only to the white coat layer of plaster. (which includes primer/sealer and paint applied to the white coat layer) Spackling compound will not adhere durably to plaster brown coat, lath boards, lath rock or wire screen.

Painter's Putty

Painter's putty is used to fill nail set holes and small nail-sized holes in wood trim. It can also be used to fill the gap between mitered pieces of wood trim. Apply flush to the surface and not beyond the boundary of the hole or gap.

(See USING PAINTER'S PUTTY TO FILL NAIL SETS AND MITER GAPS ON WOOD SURFACES, *on Page 85)*

Wood Filler

Wood filler is a thick material that can be used to fill holes and indentations in wood trim surfaces. A two-part wood filler is recommended for repairs that will bear the load of a screw or nail.

(See REPAIRING HOLES AND INDENTATIONS IN WOOD SURFACES WITH WOOD FILLER, *on Page 120)*

Wall Repair Patch

A wall repair patch can be used to cover holes and damaged areas in ceiling and wall surfaces.
(See Repairing Holes and Damaged Areas With a Wall Repair Patch, starting on Page 115)

Latex Caulk

Apply paintable latex caulk with a caulk gun to fill gaps between surface areas and wood trim. Small gaps between mitered or joined pieces of wood trim can also be filled with caulk.
(See Caulking, starting on Page 95)

Adhesive Caulk

Adhesive caulk provides greater bonding strength than regular caulk. It helps to keep caulked gaps from reappearing. Use a paintable adhesive caulk to fill the gaps between surface areas and crown molding.

Undercoater or Underbody Primer

An undercoater or underbody primer can be used to prime bare (new) trim wood or previoulsy-painted trim that is free of wood knots.

Most stain-sealing oil-based (alkyd) undercoater and underbody primers can be used to prime and seal new or previously-painted wood trim that has surface stains other than wood knots.

Undercoater and underbody primers are available that can be used as a barrier coat between layers (substrates) of oil-based and latex paint.
(See Undercoater, on Page 100)
(For information on a "barrier coat," See Primer/sealer, on Page 100)

Oil-Based Quick-drying Primer/Sealer

Oil-based quick-drying primer/sealers are ideal for priming and sealing surfaces with stains other than wood knots. Most dry in approximately two hours. Some oil-based quick-drying primer/sealers can also be used as a "barrier coat" between layers (substrates) of latex and oil-based paints.

An oil-based quick-drying primer/sealer is ideal for priming and sealing surfaces that have been repaired with joint compound, plastering materials, lightweight spackling compound or spackling compound. It is also recommended for priming and sealing surfaces after wallpaper and border removal.

Use a high quality latex primer/sealer if oil-based products are no longer available in your area.
(See Priming and sealing, on Page 100)

White-Pigmented Shellac

White-Pigmented Shellac is used to seal the toughest stains. Use it to seal wood knots, wood tannin and stains that bleed through oil-based or latex primer/sealers. (See White-Pigmented Shellac, on Page 100)

Chapter 2 Introduction to Materials and Supplies

Surface Prep Tip

Stirring primers and paints

Why thorough stirring is important: Primers and paints are comprised of ingredients that must be thoroughly mixed to ensure optimum product performance. Ingredients often separate within the can, as lighter ingredients rise to the top while heavier ones fall to the bottom. The ingredients that fall to the bottom may collect and become solid. For best results, recently purchased primers and paints should be thoroughly stirred, even when they are placed in the paint shaker at the paint store or home center.

Stored primers and paints may require additional stirring. They may also need to be strained to remove any pieces of dried paint film or particles from storage or previous use.

If you are not sure if a can of stored primer or paint is usable, take it to your paint dealer.

Thorough stirring: Using a stirring stick, stir from the bottom of the can to the top of the can with a circular motion. The bottom-to-top circular motion will blend any ingredients that have separated within the can. You may first have to drag the stick across the bottom to dislodge any solids. Stir until all solids are dissolved, and the material has a uniform look and feel.

Testing for thorough stirring: Test for thorough stirring by holding the stirring stick straight-up-and-down in the middle of the can. Allowing the stick to touch the bottom, move the stick slowly from left-to-right several times. If you feel the stick move across any solids, or if it seems to drag towards the bottom, then solids are still concentrated at, or near, the bottom of the can. Continue stirring until you can move the stick along the bottom without feeling any solids or bottom drag. After stirring, remove the stick and check it for solids. If solids are found on the stirring stick, place the stick back into the can and continue stirring until the solids are dissolved. If particles or solids are still present after repeated stirring (several minutes), discard previously stored primer or paint in accordance with local law. *(See Surface Prep Tip below)*

If your can of recently-purchased primer or paint has particles or solids that will not dissolve after through stirring, return it to the dealer for a refund or exchange.

Surface Prep Tip

Disposing of primers, paints, materials and supplies

For information regarding the safe disposal of primers, paints, materials and supplies, call your local Solid Waste Authority.

Dispose of all surface preparation and painting refuse in accordance with local law.

For information regarding the proper disposal of anything pertaining to surface preparation, house painting or home repair, contact your local Solid Waste Authority.

Supplies

Empty metal paint can

You will need several empty one-gallon metal paint cans for your surface preparation and painting project. They are useful for several surface preparation and painting tasks. Use an empty metal can for holding small portions of primer, primer/sealer, White-Pigmented Shellac, or paint for application with a paintbrush. A one-gallon can filled with about an inch of water will be needed for the caulking method covered in *Chapter 5, starting on Page 95*. A metal paint can with a lid will be needed for the safe disposal of any solvent-moistened wiping rags or towels. *(See AVOIDING SPONTANEOUS COMBUSTION FIRE, on Page 24)*

Your local paint store and home center have empty one-gallon paint cans for sale. Be sure to get a handle and lid for each can purchased.

Plastic

Plastic can be used to cover furniture, cabinets, counters and masonry areas. It can also be used to seal room entrances before surface sanding.

DO NOT apply or use any solvent-based surface preparation materials or supplies in a room or area that has been sealed with plastic. Apply and use solvent-based surface preparation materials and supplies only in rooms and areas with proper ventilation.

Surface Prep Tip

Cover furniture with two sheets of plastic

During work area cleanup, the removal of plastic often releases sanding dust into the air. Keep furniture protected from airborne sanding dust by covering furniture within the work area with two sheets of plastic. Remove the top piece of plastic and allow any airborne dust to settle for an hour or so before removing the bottom piece. This tip will help to keep your furniture clean.

MASKING TAPES USED IN SURFACE PREPARATION AND PAINTING

Preparing the work area for surface preparation and painting involves covering and protecting several different types of surfaces. The finish on some surfaces can tolerate a masking tape with a strong adhesive, while the finish on other surfaces may be damaged unless a masking tape with a lower adhesive strength is used.

Today, tape manufacturers provide a wide variety of masking tapes that can be used when preparing and painting surfaces. These "painting masking tapes" vary in color and adhesion strength. They are designed for application to specific surfaces for specific time periods. You will often use more than one painting masking tape during surface preparation and painting.

Based on the surfaces you need to cover and protect, a knowledgeable paint salesperson can advise you concerning the painting masking tapes that you will need for your surface preparation and painting project. Always follow the tape manufacturer's directions for use.

Before tape application, **BE SURE** that you have selected a tape that is approved for use by the manufacturer for the surface on which you will be fastening it, and know the time period, or "clean removal time," for which the tape is approved for surface application. Choosing the correct tape and knowing its clean removal time helps to prevent surface damage upon the tape's removal. Carefully remove tape from the surface before the end of the clean removal time period. Tape left fastened to surfaces beyond the clean removal time may harden, leaving an adhesive residue. It may also cause surface damage upon removal. Reapply fresh tape if needed. When in doubt concerning tape selection or usage, contact the tape manufacturer.

For more information about painting masking tapes, contact a tape manufacturer. You will often find a toll-free customer information phone number on the inside of the tape roll. Ask for an information brochure, or brochures, on masking tapes that are recommended for use when preparing and painting surfaces. Brochures are available that show you the recommended tape, or tapes, for use on the surfaces you will need to cover and protect.

Lubricant

Apply a quality lubricant to the moving part of a roller frame should it begin to squeak during use. When squeaking occurs, apply a drop or two of lubricant onto the joint where the "neck" of the tool meets the roller. Lubrication will help to keep your roller frame operating at peak efficiency, and prevent annoying squeaks.

Adhesive Remover

Use an adhesive remover to clean the residue left by the removal of stickers, masking tape, clear tape, contact paper, and other adhesive-backed items. The adhesive residue left by contact paper-like borders can also be removed using adhesive remover.

Tri-Sodium Phosphate Cleaner "TSP"

TSP is recommended for cleaning soiled surfaces before interior surface preparation and painting. When used as directed, cleaning with TSP will not leave a residue that would inhibit the adhesion of repair materials, repair compounds, primer or paint. Phosphate-free TSP Substitute, or TSP 90, can be purchased and used in states where phosphate use is banned.

Wallpaper Paste Remover

Use a wallpaper paste removing product to clean the wallpaper paste residue left after wallpaper and border removal. Wallpaper paste removers are available in both a liquid and gel.

Hand Cleaner

Hand cleaner can be used to remove surface preparation materials and solvent-based primers and paints from hands and skin.

Wiping Cloths

Wiping cloths are used for a variety of surface preparation and painting tasks. They are often used to remove dust from surfaces before the application of repair material, primer and paint. A wiping cloth is also used to remove any excess water from surfaces after wet-brush caulking. Bags and/or boxes of cotton wiping cloths are available at most paint stores and home centers. A cotton cloth or old cotton towel can also be used as a wiping cloth. Old cotton "T" shirts can be cut with scissors to make wiping cloths.

Denatured Alcohol

Denatured alcohol can be used to clean a paintbrush after the application of White-Pigmented Shellac.

Paint Thinner

Paint thinner can be used to clean paintbrushes, empty paint cans, rolling pans and roller frames after the application of oil-based materials, such as primers, primer/sealers, undercoaters and paints. If specified by the manufacturer, oil-based materials may be thinned to a more applicable consistency using paint thinner.

DO NOT use paint thinner, turpentine, mineral spirits or denatured alcohol to clean hands or skin.

Work gloves

Work gloves can be worn to protect hands during surface preparation tasks. Light work gloves can be worn to protect hands when sanding, and during tool use. Wear work gloves to protect hands when cleaning up the work area.

(See Hand protection, on Page 21)

Chemical-resistant rubber work gloves

Wear chemical-resistant rubber work gloves to protect hands when washing surfaces. They should also be worn when removing wallpaper paste residue with a wallpaper stripper or paste removing cleaner.

Wear chemical-resistant rubber work gloves when applying a paint deglosser, or when using a paint removing product.

(See Hand protection, on Page 21)
(See Clean soiled surfaces, on Page 45 and Clean mildewed surfaces, on Page 46)
(See Cleaning Wallpaper and Border Paste Residue, on Page 49)

Paint Deglosser

A paint deglosser promotes the adhesion of paint on gloss-finish-painted surfaces without manual sanding that causes sanding dust. Some paint deglossers also clean the surface.

(See Dustless Sanding, on Page 92)

Tasks to Complete Before Surface Preparation Begins

CHAPTER 3

Ceiling, wall and trim surfaces may need work or repair before surface preparation begins. Your careful inspection of these surfaces may show the need to complete one or more of the tasks listed in *Table 3.1, on page 40.* If so, complete the tasks you are capable of completing, and hire licensed professional contractors to complete any remaining tasks. Always begin this phase of the project in advance of your desired surface preparation start date, as work and repairs requiring licensed professional contractors may need to be scheduled a week or more ahead.

Surface Prep Tip

When to consult with a professional

If you are uncertain about the condition of a surface or how to make it ready for surface preparation, consult with a paint manufacturing company's representative, or a licensed professional contractor.

If you are unqualified or unable to safely or properly complete any task presented in this chapter, hire a licensed professional contractor.

Surface Prep Tip

Getting the job right the first time

Top-quality surface preparation can begin when surfaces are:

- In good repair.
- Free of wallpaper, borders, wallpaper paste and wallpaper paste residue.
- Clean.

Topics covered in Chapter 3
Tasks to complete before surface preparation begins

		Page(s)
1.	Locate and repair water leaks	43
2.	Repair water-damaged surfaces	43
3.	Replace damaged wood trim	43
4.	Remove wallpaper and borders	44
5.	Clean wallpaper and border paste residue	45, 49
6.	Clean soiled surfaces	45
7.	Clean mildewed surfaces	46
8.	Remove mold from surfaces	47
9.	Have a plasterer inspect plaster surfaces and repair plaster surface damage	47
10.	Hire a drywall contractor to replace damaged drywall	48

Table 3.1

CHAPTER 3 OBJECTIVES

1. Make a list of the tasks that need to be completed before surface preparation can begin on your project.

2. Determine the pre-surface preparation tasks that you are able to complete.

3. Hire licensed professional contractors for any tasks that you are unable to complete.

4. Complete all pre-surface preparation tasks.

Signs of water leakage and water damage		
DRYWALL SURFACES	**PLASTER SURFACES**	**WOOD SURFACES**
◊ Wetness	◊ Wetness	◊ Wetness
◊ Rust-colored spots, lines or rings	◊ Rust-colored spots, lines or rings	◊ Softness
◊ Softness	◊ Cracking and loose areas of plaster	◊ Cracking
◊ Bowing	◊ A white powdery residue called "Efflorescence"	◊ Warping
◊ Areas of cracking or peeling paint	◊ Areas of cracking or peeling paint	◊ Areas of cracking or peeling paint

Table 3.2

Tasks to Complete Before Surface Preparation Begins

1. **Locate and repair water leaks**

    Refer to *Table 3.2* for signs of water leakage and water damage on drywall, plaster and wood surfaces. These signs often indicate a problem beneath the affected surface. A leaking roof or plumbing problem is often the cause of water damage to an interior surface. And a poorly-sealed bathtub or shower can cause water leakage and water damage to a ceiling below. If you see any signs of water leakage and water damage, hire a licensed professional contractor to repair the cause of the water leakage. All water leaks should be repaired before beginning surface preparation work.

    Roofing Contractor

    A roofing contractor should inspect your roof whenever you see any sign of water leakage or water damage in rooms directly under the roof.

    Plumbing Contractor

    A plumbing contractor should inspect the plumbing in any bathroom, kitchen, laundry room or area above, adjacent or near water-damaged surfaces.

    Carpenter or Building Contractor

    A carpenter or building contractor should inspect gutters, flashing, siding and windows if a water leak is not found as a result of a roofing and plumbing inspection. Gutters that are full of leaves and debris may cause water leakage through roof sheathing or under hangs. Water can also leak where flashing, siding or windows are damaged, or in a state of poor repair.

2. **Repair water-damaged surfaces**

    After repairs have been completed to prevent water leaks, hire a licensed professional contractor to repair water-damaged surfaces. Hire a plastering contractor to repair water-damaged plaster surfaces. A carpenter, drywall contractor, or building contractor will be needed to replace all water-damaged drywall and wood surfaces. Water-damaged surfaces do not provide a durable foundation for surface preparation materials, primer, primer/sealer or paint. They may also support the growth of mildew and mold. *(Figure 3.1, on Page 46)*

3. **Replace damaged wood trim**

    Replace any wood trim that is warped, cracked or split. Warped, cracked or split wood can not be durably repaired and, for best results, should always be replaced. Wood trim that has large indentations, holes, and areas of damage, will often need to be replaced. Consult with a licensed professional carpenter whenever you have concern about the condition of a wood trim surface.

4. **Remove wallpaper and borders**

    For best results, wallpaper and borders should be removed before surface preparation begins, as wallpaper and borders do not always provide a stable substrate for the application of repair compounds and paint. This includes wallpaper and borders that have been previously primed and/or coated with paint. The previous application of primer/sealer and/or paint over wallpaper, or a border, is no guarantee of a stable substrate.

    Absorbed moisture from the application of repair compounds and paint can cause areas of wallpaper and borders to blister, and the ends and seams to lift from the surface. Wallpaper and borders that have been coated with an oil-based primer/sealer may provide a more moisture-resistant and stable substrate than wallpaper and borders that have not been coated with primer/sealer, but even after the application of primer/sealer, wallpaper and border-covered surfaces may still experience blistering and lifting with the application of repair compounds and paint. Preparing the surface after wallpaper or a border has blistered or lifted is an arduous task that is often not worth the aggravation or lack of consistent results. Surfaces where wallpaper seams have blistered, lifted or separated, are especially difficult to prepare.

    The removal of wallpaper and borders can be one of the most time-consuming and frustrating pre-surface preparation tasks. It can also be one of the most expensive tasks to complete. And depending on the quality of the wallpaper surface preparation that was done before installation, it is also the task that can cause the most surface damage. For these reasons, in many instances, it is wise to leave the removal of wallpaper and borders to a licensed professional wallpaper removal contractor.

    If you are considering removing wallpaper and borders yourself, consult with your local paint store or home center. They will recommend a wallpaper stripping liquid or gel product, and the tools and supplies that you will need. They may even provide some how-to advice. Try a test area first. If you are successful in removing wallpaper with little, or no, damage to the surface, then you may want to continue. If you are consistently damaging the drywall cover or scoring the white-coat layer of your plaster, then you may be wise to call a wallpaper removal contractor.

    Wallpaper removal contractors have the equipment, tools and experience to remove wallpaper and borders with minimal surface damage. (when the walls were properly prepared before wallpaper installation) If your walls were not properly prepared before wallpaper was installed, there will likely be damage that will be time-consuming and/or expensive to repair. In rare instances, drywall damage after wallpaper removal may require some drywall replacement. Your best bet for a difficult removal is a qualified professional.

    Although I prefer to have wallpaper removed before surface preparation begins, in some instances, wallpaper removal will be either quite expensive, (often the case when primer/sealer and/or paint has been previously applied) or the resulting surface damage will be both time-consuming and/or expensive to repair. If faced with the situation of choosing whether or not to go ahead with a difficult (and possibly surface damaging) wallpaper removal, you will have to make the best judgment call you can. Before making such a decision, obtain the advice of your paint dealer and wallpaper removal contractor. If the drywall cover is damaged during wallpaper or border removal, see *REPAIRING DRYWALL COVER DAMAGE, on Page 152.*

5. **Clean wallpaper and border paste residue**

   Wallpaper and border removal leaves a wallpaper paste residue that must be cleaned before surface preparation begins. Surfaces should be repeatedly cleaned until all paste residue and stickiness are removed. *(See CLEANING WALLPAPER AND BORDER PASTE RESIDUE, on Page 49)*

   Note: Removal of a contact paper-like border with an adhesive backing may leave an adhesive residue. Remove any adhesive residue by wiping the surface with a clean white cloth moistened with a chemical adhesive remover. When dry, clean the area with TSP, TSP 90 or TSP Substitute, and then allow twenty-four hours drying before beginning surface preparation.

6. **Clean soiled surfaces**

   Surface soiling can prevent the durable adhesion of repair material, primer and paint. It can also bleed through and stain newly applied paint. Always clean nicotine stain, food stain, soot, soiling and surface marks with a Tri-Sodium Phosphate cleaner "TSP" before beginning surface preparation. TSP 90 or TSP Substitute can be used in states where phosphate use is banned. TSP cleaners, when used as directed, will not inhibit repair material, primer or paint adhesion.

   Walls free of soiling and marks do not need to be cleaned, but should be wiped with a cloth or towel to remove any visible dust or cobwebs.

   When using TSP, TSP 90 or TSP Substitute

   Read and follow the directions for use and safety precautions printed on the container. Wear eye protection, chemical-resistant rubber gloves and a long-sleeve shirt during application. A double-layer of drop cloths should be used to protect flooring surfaces. Rinse skin and flooring surfaces with water should contact be made with the TSP cleaning solution. Allow 24 hours for cleaned surfaces to dry before beginning surface preparation. Humid conditions may lengthen drying time.

Surface Prep Tip

Removing adhesive residue from clear tapes, masking tapes and stickers.

The glue-like adhesive found on clear tapes and masking tapes is often difficult to clean. Adhesive residue from stickers can also be difficult to remove. Sanding may remove dried adhesive residue, but is often unsuccessful in removing gummier residue.

Use an adhesive remover to remove adhesive residue from painted surfaces. After the residue has been removed and the surface is dry, wash the surface with TSP, TSP 90 or TSP Substitute. Rinse and allow 24 hours for washed surfaces to dry. Humid conditions may lengthen drying.

DO NOT mix bleach with ammonia or any ammonia-based cleaning product.

Figure 3.1
Water-damaged and mildewed drywall.

7. **Clean mildewed surfaces**

   Mildewed surfaces can be cleaned with a solution of bleach and water. Mix 3/4 cup of bleach with every gallon of water. Wipe surfaces with a fresh cloth and clean water to rinse after mildew has been removed. Wear eye protection, long sleeved shirt and chemical-resistant rubber work gloves when cleaning mildewed surfaces.

   When cleaning surfaces, a double-layer of drop cloths should be used to protect flooring surfaces. Rinse skin and flooring surfaces with water should contact be made with the cleaning solution. Allow 24 hours for surfaces to dry before beginning surface preparation. Humid conditions may lengthen drying time.

   For information about mildew, log onto the Centers for Disease Control and Prevention (CDC) website: www.cdc.gov. In the search box, type in the word "mildew."

   When mildew growth requires drywall replacement

   The presence of mildew requires drywall replacement once mildew has penetrated the drywall. *(Figure 3.1)* Humid conditions and absorbed water will often promote mildew growth on, or within, drywall. Mildew forming on the surface may penetrate the drywall through cracked or peeling paint. A water leak can cause mildew growth on the unprotected backside of the drywall. When mildew has penetrated the drywall surface from either the front or back, it may not be possible to kill all resident mildew by surface cleaning. Replace drywall that has visible surface mildew penetration. Drywall that has absorbed moisture due to a water leak should also be replaced.

   Note: Turning on your bathroom vent fan during showering and bathing will help to prevent moisture damage and the formation of mildew on bathroom surfaces. A vent fan should be installed in every bathroom that has a shower or bathtub.

8. **Remove mold from surfaces**

    Remove mold from surfaces before surface preparation work begins. Mold-damaged surfaces, and areas where mold has become established, need to be replaced or professionally remediated. Attempting to clean, prepare or repair mold-damaged surfaces, or areas where mold has become established, can result in the spreading of mold spores throughout your home. Breathing mold spores can cause sickness. Contact a licensed professional mold remediation contractor if you have, or suspect, the presence of mold on, or within, the painted and finished surfaces of your home.

    For more information about mold, log onto the Centers for Disease Control and Prevention (CDC) website: www.cdc.gov. In the search box, type in the word "mold."

9. **Have a licensed professional plastering contractor inspect plaster surfaces and repair any plaster surface damage**

    If you own a home with plaster surfaces, you need to know a good plastering contractor. Plaster surfaces are more complex and difficult to repair than drywall surfaces. They also tend to sag and bow with age. It is wise to have your home's plaster surfaces inspected by a plastering contractor before beginning surface preparation work. Follow the advice of your plasterer and have him complete any needed repairs. Be sure to ask the plasterer for the curing time of completed repairs, and allow repairs to cure for the time specified before beginning surface preparation.

    Author's note about plaster surface preparation and repair

    With respect to plaster surfaces, the scope of this book is limited to the preparation of the white coat layer only. White coat is the smooth, outermost layer of the plaster surface. It accepts primer/sealer and paint. When in good overall condition, small holes, indentations and cracks in white coat can be repaired with good results. When plaster damage extends below the white coat layer into the brown coat layer, lath boards, lath rock or wire screen, it is time to call a licensed professional plastering contractor. Plaster patching and repair products are available, but achieving consistently good plaster repair results may be difficult for the non-professional.

    Applying decorative paint, faux finish, mural paint or stencils over plaster surfaces with peeling paint

    Plaster surfaces that have areas of peeling paint may not be suitable for the durable application of decorative paint, faux finish, mural art or stencils. Peeling paint on plaster ceiling and wall surfaces can indicate a paint adhesion problem that occurs due to lime precipitating out of the white coat layer of the plaster surface. This situation, called plaster "efflorescence," can be detected by running your finger over the surface were paint has peeled. If your finger picks up a white coating or powdery residue, then the plaster has a lime precipitate. Surfaces with a lime precipitate will likely continue to have poor paint adhesion, even after thorough surface preparation. For best results, locate your decorative paint, faux finish, mural art and stencil art on plaster ceiling and wall surfaces that are in good condition with good current paint adhesion.

    Repaired sections of damaged plaster (repaired by a plasterer) which had areas of peeling paint can be suitable for decorative paint, faux finish, mural art, and stencil art application, if the surface around the repair has good paint adhesion. After the repair has cured, prime the repair and the rest of the ceiling or wall surface (where the repair is located) with oil-based primer/sealer before paint application.

(See PRIMING AND SEALING SITUATIONS: New or repaired plaster, on Page 101)
(See Before the application of decorative paint, faux finish, mural art and stencils, on Page 102)

10. Hire a licensed professional drywall contractor to replace damaged drywall

CLEANING WALLPAPER AND BORDER PASTE RESIDUE

Tools and materials

Eye and respiratory system protection, chemical-resistant rubber work gloves, long sleeve work shirt, cleaning pail or bucket, cleaning cloths, drop cloths, wallpaper stripper or wallpaper paste remover.

Steps

Cover flooring surfaces with a double-layer of drop cloths. A drop cloth can be folded in-half and placed along the base of the wall.

1. Wear eye protection and any recommended respiratory system protection, a long sleeve shirt, and chemical-resistant rubber work gloves.
   (*See Pages 19-20 for eye and respiratory system protection information*)

2. Read and follow the directions on the container of wallpaper stripper or wallpaper paste remover. Mix as directed.

3. Wash and rinse all areas of wallpaper paste until clean. Also wash and rinse six inches onto the ceiling, and all wood trim surfaces that the cleaning solution or paste come in contact with. *(Fig. 3.2)* Use a 6" taping knife to gently remove any remaining clumps of paste and pieces of wallpaper or border. Work carefully with the taping knife to avoid gouging, tearing or scratching the surface.

Figure 3.2
Wash six inches onto the ceiling to remove any paste residual beyond the wall.

4. Allow drying. A gritty haze will remain after drying.

5. Re-clean and rinse any areas that are sticky, or that have remaining paste residue.

6. Remove the dried haze by sanding the surface using a pole sander with 80-grit pole sander paper. Smaller areas can be sanded using a sanding sponge.

7. Remove sanding dust with a wiping cloth or towel. Slightly dampening the wiping cloth or towel will help to control dust. Allow any surface moisture to dry before beginning surface preparation.
   Note: During surface preparation, oil-based primer/sealer should be applied to all surfaces where wallpaper and borders have been removed.
   (*See Page 101 for priming and sealing information*)

Workplace Lighting

Purchasing good workplace lighting is one of the most important investments that can be made when looking to improve the quality of your interior house painting surface preparation. Professional-grade lighting is as important as the use of professional-grade tools and paintbrushes. The best surface preparation and painting results are only possible when you have the advantage of good lighting.

End table lamps and clamp lights just do not provide the illumination necessary for top-quality surface preparation and painting work. If that is what you have been using, do yourself a favor and purchase a good work light after reading this chapter.

WORK LIGHTS

Proper lighting of the work area helps you to accurately view and successfully complete surface preparation tasks. Good work lights are valuable and necessary tools. For surface preparation and painting, use halogen work lights.

Twin head halogen work light

The twin head halogen work light *(Fig. 4.1)* has two lights, an adjustable pole and a tripod base. Most twin head halogen work lights have a 500-Watt halogen light bulb in each light head. 500-Watt halogen light bulbs provide greater lighting brightness and a much larger area of illumination than standard light bulbs (used in house lamps and clamp lights). An adjustable pole enables the light heads to be raised or lowered for illumination on surfaces both high and low. The tripod base is adjustable to provide needed stability. The two light heads can be used together to focus light in one direction. They can also be moved independently of each other to vary the amount of light in one area, or to illuminate a wider surface area. Light heads can be adjusted backward for work on high walls or ceilings, and forward for work on low wall areas and baseboards.

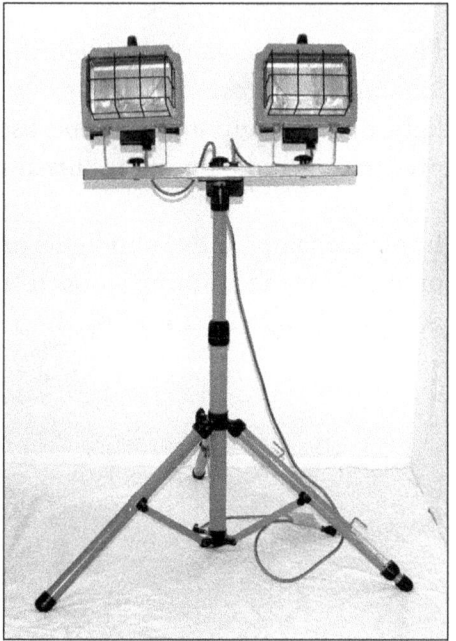

Figure 4.1
Twin head halogen work light.

Surface preparation work in large rooms, or in rooms with high ceilings, may require two twin head halogen work lights. If two twin head halogen work lights are needed, operate each light on electricity from its own room or area. Two twin head halogen work lights may blow a fuse or trip a breaker if they are operated on electricity from the same room or area. Use a separate heavy-gauge extension cord for each light.

Note: The terms "head" and "light head" refer to the unit comprising the light housing, halogen light bulb, safety cage (over the light bulb) and the positioning handle used to move each head.

Single head halogen work light

Single head halogen work lights *(Fig. 4.2)* are available for lighting small areas, such as hallways, bathrooms and closets. These work lights rest on their base several inches above the floor. They can be adjusted to aim light for work on ceilings. Single head halogen work lights that have a tripod base and adjustable pole are also available.

Figure 4.2
Small single head halogen work light.

- **DO NOT leave lit or hot work lights unattended.**
- **Before leaving the work area, unplug work lights and allow them to cool for several minutes.**
- **Touching the light head housing or metal cage covering the lights while the work light is lit or hot can cause burns to skin.**
- **Keep work lights at a safe distance from ceiling, wall and trim surfaces.**
- **Also keep work lights at a safe distance from all flammable materials and objects.**
- **Follow the directions for use and safety guidelines from the light's manufacturer.**

SECTION II

Surface Preparation Techniques and Repairs

Surface Preparation Techniques

Surface preparation techniques are the basic skills needed to prepare interior surfaces. They require skill with surface preparation tools, and knowledge of surface preparation repair compounds and materials. You will use several surface preparation techniques in each room or area that you prepare for paint, decorative paint, faux finish, mural art and stencils. In a project where you are preparing several rooms, you may use most, if not all, of the surface preparation techniques covered in this chapter. Mastering surface preparation techniques will make a noticeable difference in the quality of your surface preparation. It will also help to prepare you for the common surface preparation repairs covered in *Chapter 6.* The surface preparation techniques covered in this chapter are listed in *Table 5.1, on the next page.*

Topics covered in Chapter 5
Surface Preparation Techniques

		Page
1.	Using a 6" taping knife to apply repair compounds	60
2.	Taping knife technique for flush-fills	61
3.	Tips for skillful taping knife use	62
4.	Application of drywall joint compound	64
5.	Application of lightweight spackling compound	68
6.	Application of spackling compound	72
7.	Skim coating ceiling and wall surfaces with drywall joint compound	77
8.	Skim coating wood trim surfaces with spackling compound	82
9.	Using painter's putty to fill nail sets and miter gaps on wood surfaces	85
10.	Sanding	88
11.	Caulking	95
12.	Priming and sealing	100

Table 5.1

CHAPTER 5 OBJECTIVES

1. The ability to apply repair compounds to fill small holes and indentations called "flush-fills."

2. Developing skill with the 6" taping knife and putty knife.

3. Learning about and applying repair compounds.

4. Learning the skim coating technique.

5. Using painter's putty to fill nail sets and miter gaps on wood surfaces.

6. Knowing why sanding is important to surface preparation.

7. Becoming familiar with sanding tools.

8. Developing skill with sanding tools.

9. Learning why caulking is an important surface preparation skill.

10. Mastering the wet-brush caulking technique.

11. Knowing why priming and sealing is important before the application of paint, decorative paint, faux finish and stencils.

12. Learning about the various types of primers and sealers.

13. Knowing the primer, primer/sealer or sealer to use for each surface preparation task.

14. Mastering the surface preparation techniques covered in this chapter.

Using a 6" Taping Knife to Apply Repair Compounds

The skillful application of drywall joint compound, lightweight spackling compound and spackling compound is essential to good surface preparation. This book refers to these three surface preparation materials as "repair compounds." The tool that enables skillful repair compound application is the flexible blade 6" taping knife. In this chapter, you will learn how to use the flexible blade 6" taping knife to apply repair compounds flush to the surface when filling small holes and indentations called "flush-fills." You will also learn how to apply drywall joint compound to skim coat ceiling and wall surfaces, and spackling compound to skim coat wood trim surfaces.

Using The 6" Taping Knife For Flush-Fills

The 6" taping knife is used to apply drywall joint compound and lightweight spackling compound to ceiling and wall surfaces. It can also be used to apply spackling compound on wood trim surfaces. Although this section demonstrates the application of drywall joint compound, the application method for flush-fills can also be used when applying lightweight spackling compound, spackling compound and wood filler.

Begin the method for flush-fills by using a putty knife to place a marble-sized amount of drywall joint compound on the center of your taping knife blade. *(Figure 5.1)* Keeping the blade in contact with the surface at approximately a 45-degree angle, gently pull the taping knife over the small hole or indentation. The hole or indentation should be filled once the blade has passed. Remove excess joint compound by pulling the taping knife over the repair in another direction, as seen in *Diagram 5.1, on opposite page*. Continue these application and removal strokes until the hole or indentation is filled and excess joint compound has been removed. The removal of excess joint compound bordering the fill reduces needed sanding time and effort. Use your putty knife to center joint compound on your taping knife blade after every few strokes. Once you have mastered using a marble-sized amount of joint compound, try working with slightly larger amounts.

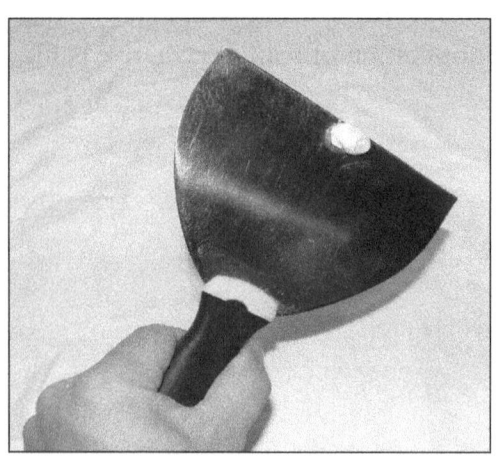

Figure 5.1
Start your flush-fill repairs with a marble-sized amount of repair compound. Pictured is drywall joint compound.

> **Small nail-sized holes in wood trim surfaces are flush-filled with painter's putty, whose use is covered later in this chapter.**

Chapter 5 Surface Preparation Techniques

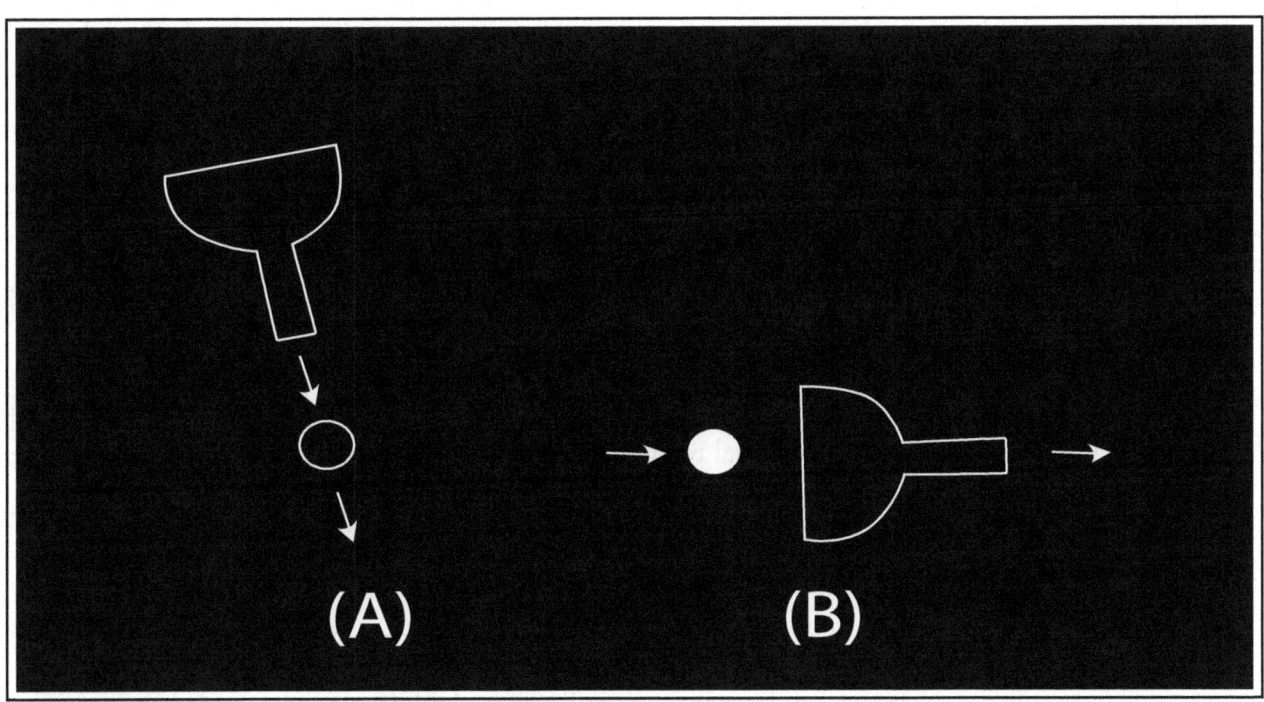

Diagram 5.1 Taping knife technique for flush-fills
Apply joint compound in one direction (A), remove excess in another direction (B). Repeat until the hole or indentation is filled and compound is flush to the surface. Joint compound outside the border of the fill should be smooth without any edges or build-ups.

TIPS FOR SKILLFUL TAPING KNIFE USE

1. **Use your taping knife and putty knife carefully**

   Taping knife and putty knife blades have sharp corners and edges that can inflict cuts and cause injuries. Carefully handle, use and clean these tools.

2. **Use a taping knife with a flexible blade**

   When applying drywall joint compound, a taping knife with a flexible blade gives you more control than a taping knife with a rigid blade. The flexible blade makes the tool more responsive to pressure exerted by the hand, which enables the user to apply joint compound efficiently and precisely. Precise joint compound application helps to reduce sanding time and effort. In the next chapter, you will learn how to use the flexible blade taping knife to shape and contour applied joint compound when crafting surface preparation repairs. *(Information about shaping and contouring applied joint compound can be found starting on Page 110)*

3. **Use the taping knife at approximately a 45-degree angle to the surface**

   At approximately a 45-degree angle to the surface, you can easily maneuver the taping knife to complete the flush-filling technique shown in *Diagram 5.1, on the previous page.*

4. **Keep your wrist flexible**

   Keeping a loose, flexible wrist is essential to good taping knife technique. Make your taping knife strokes using arm, hand and wrist action. Avoid taping knife strokes with a locked wrist.

5. **Apply joint compound with only one side of the taping knife blade**

   Applying joint compound with both sides of the taping knife blade is to be avoided, as joint compound is more likely to dry on the blade when both sides are used. Dried joint compound on the blade will often "scratch" and indent the application. And dried compound that becomes part of the application often leaves a noticeable deposit or bump on the surface. Apply joint compound with only one side of the taping knife blade, periodically using a wiping cloth to remove any compound on the back-side of the blade.

6. **Re-center joint compound after every few strokes**

   During application, joint compound will move towards the corners of the taping knife blade. If not continually re-centered, compound will "drip" or fall from the corners of the blade. Use your putty knife to re-center joint compound on your taping knife blade after every few strokes. Re-centering joint compound will help you to complete flush-fills quickly and precisely, with little, or no, material waste. *(Figures 5.2 - 5.4, on opposite page)*

7. **Gradually increase the amount of joint compound on your taping knife blade**

   After mastering the application of a marble-sized amount of joint compound, gradually increase the amount on your taping knife blade. A golf ball-sized amount is a good goal.

8. **Remove dried joint compound from the taping knife and mud tray**

   During application, joint compound may begin to dry on the taping knife and in the mud tray. Pieces of dried joint compound can cause surface imperfections in applied coats. *(See Tip 5)* They can also become part of the surface. To avoid these application problems, remove and discard any dried, or partially hardened, bits of joint compound from your taping knife and mud tray.

9. **Clean and dry the taping knife and putty knife after use**

   After use, remove joint compound from the taping knife and putty knife. Clean the taping knife and putty knife with water, and then dry with a wiping cloth or towel. Cleaning and drying these tools helps to prevent rusting and corrosion.

10. **Practice your taping knife technique: repetition brings mastery**

    Work to achieve flush-fills that have little, or no, excess application. The border of the flush-fill is usually where excess application can be found. You have achieved good results when your flush-fills require minimal sanding, and are virtually undetectable after priming and painting.

Figure 5.2
Joint compound that needs to be re-centered.

Figure 5.3
Begin to re-center joint compound by first removing it from the taping knife blade with a putty knife.

Figure 5.4
Place removed joint compound at the center of the taping knife near the tip of the blade.

Section Note:

This list of taping knife tips can also be used for the application of lightweight spackling compound and spackling compound.

Application of Drywall Joint Compound

Drywall joint compound is the most frequently used interior surface preparation repair compound. It is easy to apply, dries quickly, and can be sanded precisely. Joint compound can be applied to drywall and the white coat layer of plaster surfaces.

Tools and materials

Eye and respiratory system protection, 6" taping knife, putty knife, mud tray and joint compound, fine/medium-grit sanding sponge, wiping cloth or towel, oil-based quick-drying primer/sealer, empty paint can, "all paints" paintbrush, paint thinner and hand cleaner.

Steps

1. Wear eye and respiratory system protection.
   (See Pages 19-20 for eye and respiratory system protection information)

2. Use the medium-grit side of a sanding sponge or 80-grit sandpaper to sand the border of any hole or indentation you will fill with joint compound.

3. Remove sanding dust with a wiping cloth or towel. Slightly dampening the wiping cloth or towel will help to control dust. Allow any surface moisture to dry before going to *Step 4*.

4. Use a putty knife to load joint compound into a mud tray. Start with a small amount, as leftover joint compound should be discarded. A cup of joint compound is a good starting amount. It should be enough to fill the small holes and indentations in several rooms.

5. Use a putty knife to center a marble-sized amount of joint compound on the end of your 6" taping knife blade. *(Figure 5.1, on Page 60)* Apply joint compound in one direction and remove excess by pulling the taping knife across the surface in another direction. *(See Diagram 5.1, on Page 61)* Repeat until the fill is flush to the surface. Any joint compound outside the border of the fill should be smooth without any edges or build-ups.

   Note: A flexible blade putty knife or flexible blade 4" taping knife can also be used to apply joint compound.

6. Allow drying. Joint compound is dry when uniformly white.

7. Apply a second coat of joint compound. Allow drying.

8. If necessary, apply a third coat of joint compound to bring the repair flush to the surface. A little extra compound can be applied just past flush to allow for shrinkage and sanding. Allow drying.

9. When dry, lightly sand the fill with the fine-grit side of a fine/medium sanding sponge.

10. Remove sanding dust with a wiping cloth or towel. *(See Wiping Cloths, on Page 34)* Slightly dampening the wiping cloth or towel will help to control dust. Allow any surface moisture to dry before going to *Step 11*.

11. Stir then pour oil-based quick-drying primer/sealer into an empty paint can. An inch or two in the paint can will usually be enough to prime the filled holes and indentations in several rooms. Apply a coat of oil-based quick-drying primer/sealer over completed repairs. A roller frame, 3/8" nap roller cover, rolling pan and extension rolling pole can be used to apply primer/sealer over large areas or entire ceiling and wall surfaces. Primer/sealer can be applied to smaller areas with a slim roller frame and cover, *(See Slim roller frame and cover in Figure 5.42, on Page 105)* or a paintbrush. Allow drying.

    Note: If oil-based products are no longer available in your area, use a high-quality latex primer/sealer capable of priming and sealing drywall joint compound in this step. Follow directions for cleaning tools, hands and skin. Wear any recommended respiratory system protection.

    Note: If other preparation or repair work will be done, then apply primer/sealer in this room or part of the project after all preparation and repair work has been completed.

12. Lightly sand dried primer/sealer with the fine-grit side of a fine/medium sanding sponge. Larger areas can be sanded using a pole sander with 100-grit or 120-grit pole sander paper.

13. Remove sanding dust with a wiping cloth or towel. Slightly dampening the wiping cloth or towel will help to control dust. Allow any surface moisture to dry before going to *Step 14*.

14. Apply paint, decorative paint, faux finish or stencil.

Refer to Chapter 1 for information regarding safety and avoiding spontaneous combustion fire when using paint thinner, turpentine, mineral spirits, denatured alcohol, paint deglosser, oil-based primers and primer/sealers and White-Pigmented Shellac.

Estimated Time to Complete this Technique

The estimated time to complete the method steps for the application of joint compound to fill nail-sized holes and small indentations in a room is less than four hours. The actual working time will usually be about a minute for each indentation or hole filled. For greatest efficiency, perform joint compounding repairs in several rooms simultaneously.

Note: Estimated time to complete method steps includes drying times for repair compounds and primer/sealer. Refer to the directions on the container for drying times of repair compounds and primer/sealer. Humid conditions will lengthen drying times. Other preparation and repair work can be done in the room while waiting for repair compounds to dry.

Tips and Troubleshooting

Application of Drywall Joint Compound

1. Apply drywall joint compound using a taping knife with a flexible blade. Taping knives with rigid blades do not provide enough dexterity for precise application.

2. Apply joint compound in thin, even coats to avoid the formation of air bubbles, air holes and cracks during drying. If air bubbles, air holes or cracks form after application, reduce the thickness of future applications.

3. Remove excess joint compound application, edge lines and build-ups (build-ups are areas of compound that are not smooth and uniform). Excess application and build-ups around the edges of the fill, and outside the border of the fill, will require additional sanding time and effort. Correctly applied joint compound will begin to dry at the edges in just a few minutes.

4. The application of joint compound can help to reduce, or eliminate, "cosmetic" defects caused by past surface preparation and painting. Cosmetic defects do not need to be "repaired," but they do need to be concealed to give the surface a smooth and uniform appearance. These cosmetic defects include the visible outline of poorly-sanded flush-fills and repairs. They also include excessive roller cover nap pattern, roller cover tracking lines, paintbrush bristle marks and paint drips. Joint compound should be applied to conceal these cosmetic defects. Areas of cosmetic defects can also be skim coated. *(See Skim coating, on Page 76)*

5. For best results, discard the leftover joint compound in your mud tray. Leftover joint compound is often sprinkled with bits of surface debris and pieces of dried joint compound from the sides of the mud tray. These pieces of surface debris and dried joint compound cause scratch marks and leave debris in later applications.

6. Keep the inside of the joint compound container clean and a layer of plastic on the top of the joint compound during storage. The layer of plastic helps keep the joint compound from drying inside the container.

7. Regular weight joint compound shrinks a little more as it dries than lightweight joint compound, but is often easier to sand.

8. Store joint compound at room temperature. Do not allow it to freeze. Joint compound should not be used if it has partially hardened, been exposed to freezing, or has a foul odor.

9. After three, or so, full coats of joint compound are applied to "non-flush" surface preparation repairs, *(See Chapter 6)* try the application of partial coats of joint compound to fill any remaining holes, indentations or areas that need additional filling or contouring. Partial coats, even small spot applications, are a great way to complete and smooth the repair. I will often use partial, or spot, applications specifically to smooth the repair and reduce sanding time.

Surface Prep Tip

Applying repair compounds

A few helpful tips about applying repair compounds:

1. Drywall joint compound, lightweight spackling compound and spackling compound each have their own texture and consistency. Experimenting with each will help you to find the right amount to load onto your 6" taping knife for application. You will likely find that it is easier to work with smaller amounts of lightweight spackling compound than spackling compound or drywall joint compound.

2. A flexible blade putty knife or a flexible blade 4" taping knife can be used to apply repair compounds into small or tight spaces.

3. Humid conditions will lengthen repair compound drying times. Allow compounds to dry before re-coating or sanding.

4. Repair compounds often shrink between coats. Lightweight spackling compound shrinks the least, if at all, while joint compound shrinks the most. To compensate for shrinkage, and to allow for sanding, it is acceptable to apply a little extra repair compound to fill a hole or indentation past "flush." Careful sanding will bring the repair flush to the surface.

5. The application of excessive thicknesses of joint compound or spackling compound in one coat will result in cracking of the applied material during drying. Avoid excessive applications and follow directions concerning the layering of deep fills.

APPLICATION OF LIGHTWEIGHT SPACKLING COMPOUND

Lightweight spackling compound is a unique repair material. It has a light consistency, resists sagging, and shrinks little, if any, during drying. These qualities enable lightweight spackling compound to fill holes and indentations, often in just one application. It can be used to fill larger surface preparation holes and indentations in ceiling and wall surfaces, such as the ones made by electricians. *(See Figures 5.5 - 5.7)* Lightweight spackling compound can be used on drywall, the white coat layer of plaster and wood.

Tools and materials

Eye and respiratory system protection, 6" taping knife, putty knife, scraper, mud tray and lightweight spackling compound, fine/medium-grit sanding sponge, wiping cloth or towel, oil-based quick-drying primer/sealer, empty paint can, "all paints" paintbrush, paint thinner and hand cleaner.

Steps

1. Wear eye and respiratory system protection. *(See Pages 19-20 for eye and respiratory system protection information)*

2. Use a putty knife or scraper to remove any loose material from the hole or indentation. Then sand the repair area with the medium-grit side of a sanding sponge or 80-grit sandpaper.

3. Remove sanding dust and debris from the hole or indentation with a duster. A painting duster can be made by sawing the handle off an old paintbrush. *(See Duster in Figure 6.33, on Page 145)*

   Remove sanding dust from the border and area around the hole or indentation with a wiping cloth or towel. Slightly dampening the wiping cloth or towel will help to control dust. Allow any surface moisture to dry before going to *Step 4*.

4. Use a flexible blade putty knife, flexible blade 4" taping knife or flexible blade 6" taping knife to apply

Figure 5.5
Filled hole measures approximately 1½" wide and 1¼" high. The depth of the hole measures ½".

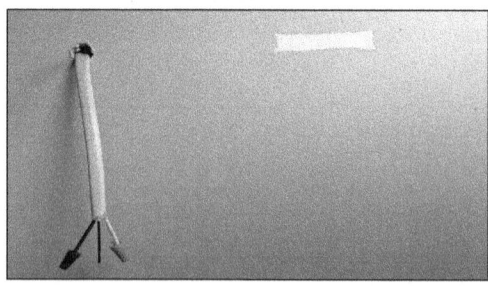

Figure 5.6
Rectangular opening made by electrician for pulling wiring during renovation is filled with lightweight spackling compound. Opening measures approximately 3" wide by ¾" high. (See picture -center top)

DO NOT fill any hole where wiring has been installed. (See picture -top left)

lightweight spackling compound into the hole or indentation. Lightweight spackling compound should be applied flush to the surface. Remove excess. *(Figure 5.7)*

5. Allow drying as per instructions on the container.

6. Lightweight spackling compound may shrink slightly during drying. If shrinkage occurs, apply a second coat of lightweight spackling to bring the repair area flush to the surface. Allow drying.

7. Lightly sand the repair with the fine-grit side of a sanding sponge.

8. Remove sanding dust with a wiping cloth or towel. Slightly dampening the wiping cloth or towel will help to control dust. Allow any surface moisture to dry before going to *Step 9*.

9. Stir then pour oil-based quick-drying primer/sealer into an empty paint can. An inch or two in the paint can will usually be enough to prime the filled holes and indentations in several rooms. Apply a coat of oil-based quick-drying primer/sealer over completed repairs. A roller frame, 3/8" nap roller cover, rolling pan and extension rolling pole can be used to apply primer/sealer over large areas or entire ceiling and wall surfaces. Primer/sealer can be applied to smaller areas with a slim roller frame and cover, or a paintbrush. Allow drying.

   Note: If oil-based products are no longer available in your area, use a high-quality latex primer/sealer capable of priming and sealing lightweight spackling in this step. Follow directions for cleaning tools, hands and skin. Wear any recommended respiratory system protection.

   Note: If other preparation or repair work will be done, then apply primer/sealer in this room or part of the project after all preparation and repair work has been completed.

10. Lightly sand dried primer/sealer with the fine-grit side of a fine/medium sanding sponge. Larger areas can be sanded using a pole sander with 100-grit or 120-grit pole sander sandpaper.

11. Remove sanding dust with a wiping cloth or towel. Slightly dampening the wiping cloth or towel will help to control dust. Allow any surface moisture to dry before going to *Step 12*.

12. Apply paint, decorative paint, faux finish or stencil.

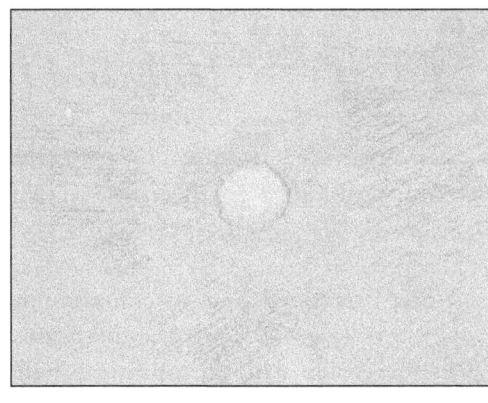

Figure 5.7
Lightweight spackling compound applied flush to the surface. The indentation measures approximately 3/4" in diameter.

Refer to Chapter 1 for information regarding safety and avoiding spontaneous combustion fire when using paint thinner, turpentine, mineral spirits, denatured alcohol, paint deglosser, oil-based primers and primer/sealers and White-Pigmented Shellac.

Estimated Time to Complete this Technique

The estimated time to complete the method steps for the application of lightweight spackling compound in a room is less than four hours. The actual working time will usually be a few minutes for each fill.

Note: Estimated time to complete method steps includes drying times for repair compounds and primer/sealer. Refer to the directions on the container for drying times of repair compounds and primer/sealer. Humid conditions will lengthen drying times. Other preparation and repair work can be done in the room while waiting for repair compounds to dry.

TIPS AND TROUBLESHOOTING

Application of Lightweight Spackling Compound

1. Stir a few drops of water into lightweight spackling compound if it becomes crumbly or difficult to apply. Lightweight spackling compound can be more difficult to apply than joint compound, as its light texture can cause it to become crumbly during application. Continue stirring small amounts of water into the lightweight spackling compound until a more applicable consistency is achieved.

2. Filling larger holes and indentations can be done using the 6" taping knife technique shown in *Diagram 5.1, on Page 61*. Some larger holes and indentations can be filled with straight strokes in one direction when applying lightweight spackling compound.

Chapter 5 Surface Preparation Techniques

Surface Prep Tip

Preparing ahead

Preparing a room for painting, decorative painting, faux finishing or stencils may require several days. When possible, prepare two or more rooms at a time for greatest efficiency. When preparation in one room is complete, painting can begin. Continue to prepare additional rooms as you wait for either preparation materials or paint to dry. Preparing ahead eliminates much of the down time lost waiting for preparation materials and paint to dry.

Surface Prep Tip

Check your work at different times of the day in varying levels of both natural and artificial light

Varying levels of light will both hide and reveal surface defects. A combination of varying levels of both artificial light from work lights, and natural light from the sun, are needed to accurately view, and successfully complete, surface preparation tasks. Adjust your halogen work light to focus varying levels of light intensity on preparation surfaces. When you do, you will be surprised at how differently you are able to view each surface. Lower levels of light gently shadow the surface and reveal imperfections, while higher levels of light may conceal some imperfections and minimize others. Turn your halogen work light off and check preparation surfaces in natural light during the course of the day. With natural light, you may see surface imperfections not visible to you with your work light. Natural light gives the human eye a greater depth perception than artificial light. The late afternoon and early evening hours present the best low-level natural light for checking preparation surfaces. Low-level natural light exposes areas that are not flush or uniform, providing you with an excellent view of surface conditions. In rooms that are not exposed to much natural light, place a table lamp on the floor a few inches away from the wall. The low-light cast on walls from the lamp will often expose surface defects. Move the lamp to several locations along each wall.

In review, inspect surfaces and your work daily in varying amounts of both artificial and natural light. This technique will greatly improve your ability to recognize surface conditions. It will also help you to complete good interior surface preparation work.

APPLICATION OF SPACKLING COMPOUND

Spackling compound is a paste-like material that dries to a hard, durable finish. It is easy to apply and can be sanded precisely using a sanding sponge or sandpaper. These characteristics make spackling compound ideal for flush-filling small holes, indentations and scratches in wood trim surfaces. It can also be used on drywall and the white coat layer of plaster surfaces. Spackling compound is the repair compound to use for skim coating wood surfaces.
(See SKIM COATING WOOD TRIM SURFACES WITH SPACKLING COMPOUND, on Page 82)

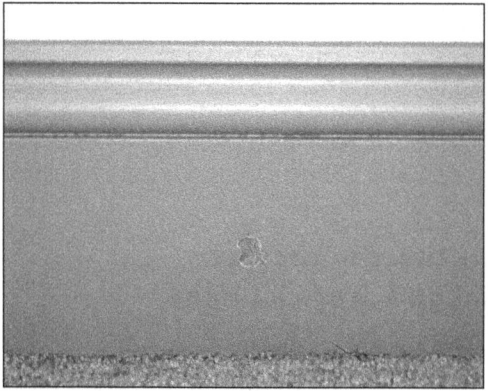

Figure 5.8
Small indentation in baseboard.

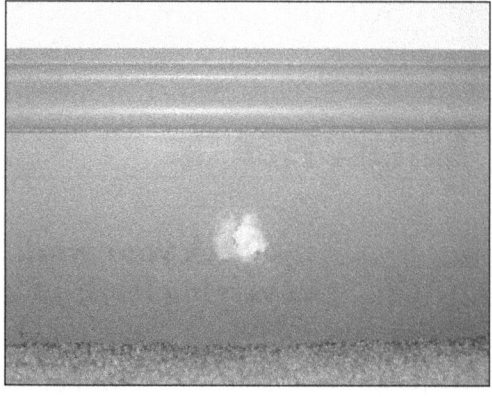

Figure 5.9
Indentation flush-filled with spackling compound. Light sanding with a sanding sponge has made the repair ready for priming.

Figure 5.10
Hammer ding in crown molding.

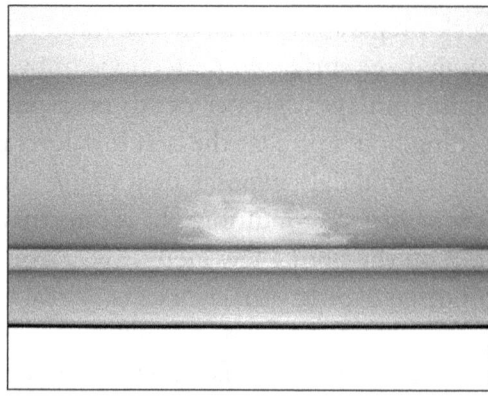

Figure 5.11
Filled ding was sanded with folded sandpaper. *(See Figure 5.12, on opposite page)* The sanded fill assumes the rounded contour of the crown molding, which will make the repair virtually undetectable when primed and painted.

Chapter 5 Surface Preparation Techniques

Tools and materials

Eye and respiratory system protection, 6" taping knife, putty knife, scraper, mud tray and spackling compound, fine/medium sanding sponge, folded 100- or 120-grit sandpaper, wiping cloth or towel, empty paint can, oil-based quick-drying primer/sealer, "all paints" paintbrush, paint thinner, hand cleaner.

Steps

1. Wear eye and respiratory system protection.
   (*See Pages 19-20 for eye and respiratory system protection information*)

2. Use a putty knife or scraper to remove any loose material from the repair area, and then sand with the medium-grit side of a sanding sponge or 80-grit sandpaper.

3. Remove sanding dust with a wiping cloth or towel. Slightly dampening the wiping cloth or towel will help to control dust. Allow any surface moisture to dry before going to *Step 4*.

4. Use a flexible blade putty knife, flexible blade 4" taping knife or flexible blade 6" taping knife to apply spackling compound to fill the hole, indentation or scratch. Spackling compound should be applied flush to the surface. Remove excess. Any spackling compound outside the fill should be smooth without any edges or build-ups.

5. Allow drying.

6. Spackling compound may shrink during drying. Apply a second coat if needed. Allow drying.

7. Lightly sand the dried repair with the fine-grit side of a sanding sponge or folded fine-grit sandpaper (100- or 120-grit).
   (*See Folding sandpaper, on Page 90*)

   Fills in curved and contoured surfaces should be sanded flush along the curve or contour. Folded sandpaper can be manipulated to enable precise, flush sanding of curved and contoured surfaces. (*Figure 5.12*)

   When curve and contour sanding, use light sanding strokes and check your progress after every two or three back-and-forth sanding passes. Do not sand the fill past flush. Re-apply spackling compound should the fill be sanded past flush, or if the contour of the fill no longer matches the contour of the surface.

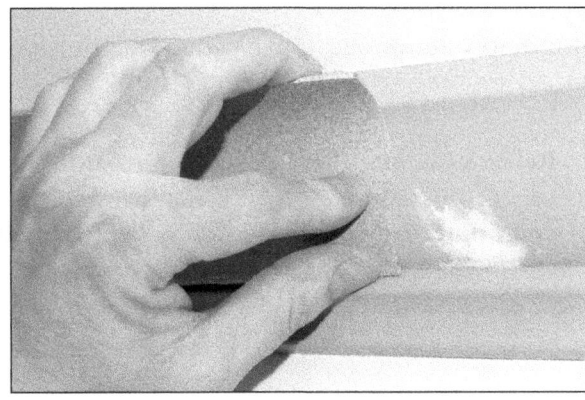

Figure 5.12
Folded sandpaper enables precise flush-fill sanding on curved portion of crown molding. On contoured surfaces, bend the sandpaper to fit the contour of the surface. The completed repair is shown in *Figure 5.11, on previous page*.

8. Remove sanding dust with a wiping cloth or towel. Slightly dampening the wiping cloth or towel will help to control dust. Allow any surface moisture to dry before going to *Step 9*.

9. Stir then pour oil-based quick-drying primer/sealer into an empty paint can. An inch or two in the paint can will usually be enough to prime the filled holes, indentations and scratches on the wood trim in several rooms. Apply a coat of oil-based quick-drying primer/sealer over completed repairs. A roller frame, 3/8" nap roller cover, rolling pan and extension rolling pole can be used to apply primer/sealer over large areas or entire ceiling and wall surfaces. Primer/sealer can be applied to smaller areas with a slim roller frame and cover, or a paintbrush. Allow drying.

    Note: If oil-based products are no longer available in your area, use a high-quality latex primer/sealer in this step. Follow directions for cleaning tools, hands and skin. Wear any recommended respiratory system protection.

    Note: If other preparation or repair work will be done, then apply primer/sealer in this room or part of the project after all preparation and repair work has been completed.

10. Lightly sand the dried primer/sealer with the fine-grit side of a sanding sponge or fine-grit sandpaper.

11. Remove sanding dust with a wiping cloth or towel. Slightly dampening the wiping cloth or towel will help to control dust. Allow any surface moisture to dry before going to *Step 12*.

12. Apply paint, decorative paint, faux finish or stencil.

Refer to Chapter 1 for information regarding safety and avoiding spontaneous combustion fire when using paint thinner, turpentine, mineral spirits, denatured alcohol, paint deglosser, oil-based primers and primer/sealers and White-Pigmented Shellac.

Chapter 5 Surface Preparation Techniques

Estimated Time to Complete this Technique

The estimated time to complete the method steps for the application of spackling compound in a room is less than four hours. The actual working time will usually be a few minutes for each fill.

Note: Estimated time to complete method steps includes drying times for repair compounds and primer/sealer. Refer to the directions on the container for drying times of repair compounds and primer/sealer. Humid conditions will lengthen drying times. Other preparation and repair work can be done in the room while waiting for repair compounds to dry.

TIPS AND TROUBLESHOOTING

Application of Spackling Compound

1. Follow the directions on the container concerning thinning should spackling compound be difficult to apply.

2. Reduce drying and sanding time with careful application of spackling compound. Removing excess spackling compound reduces the drying time of repair areas. It also reduces the sanding time and effort needed to complete repairs. Fill or conceal surface defects with smooth, even coats. Always scrape the edges of the repair to remove thick or heavy spackling compound application, edges and build-ups. *(See Figure 5.20, on Page 82)*

3. Spackling compound can be applied and formed to take the shape and contour of wood trim. Small holes, indentations and dings in the beveled, curved, rounded and detailed parts of wood trim can be filled with spackling compound. To fill holes and indentations in curved or contoured surfaces, apply spackling compound in the direction of the curve or contour. With careful sanding, the repaired wood trim can look like new.

4. Sandpaper can be cut into smaller sheets for sanding small and detailed areas of spackling compound repairs on wood trim. Cut sandpaper with scissors to the size you need.

5. Spackling compound can be used to conceal cosmetic defects on wood trim surfaces from previous surface preparation and painting. Cosmetic defects do not need to be repaired but should be concealed with spackling compound to give the surface a smooth and uniform appearance. These defects include the visible outline of poorly-sanded flush-fills and repairs. They also include paintbrush bristle marks, paint edge build ups and paint drips.

Skim coating

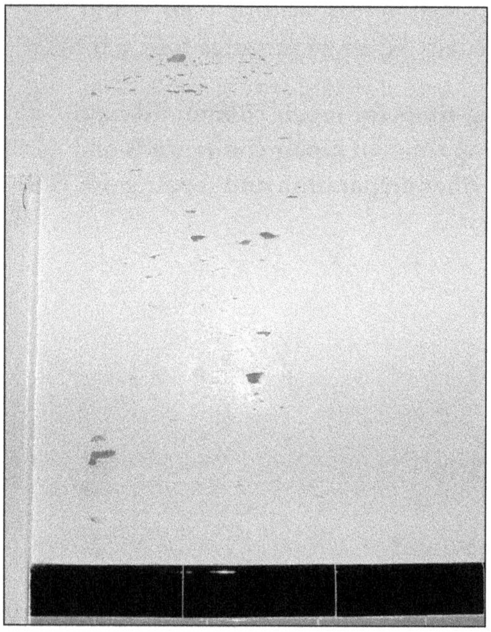

Skim coating is the technique of applying a continuous coat of a repair compound to fill and conceal multiple surface defects simultaneously. This technique is effective in restoring a smooth, uniform appearance to surfaces that are marred by minor surface damage, such as small holes, indentations and the "crater-like" areas where paint has peeled. *(Figures 5.13, to left and 5.20, on Page 82)* It can also be effective in restoring surfaces after wallpaper and border removal. *(Use with Repairing drywall cover damage, on Page 152)*

Skim coating can also help to reduce, or eliminate, the cosmetic defects that may be present from past surface preparation and painting. These defects often include edge lines from poorly-sanded repairs, excessive roller cover nap pattern, roller cover tracking lines, (tracking lines are paint build-ups made by the ends of the roller cover) paintbrush bristle marks, paint edge build ups and paint drips. Minor surface damage and cosmetic surface defects can be quickly repaired by skim coating. The skim coating technique is effective for areas both small and large. Entire ceiling and wall surfaces can be skim coated to look like new.

Skim coating is a time-saving technique. It saves you much of the time that would be required to fill or conceal surface defects individually. More time is saved during sanding, as small groups or large areas of defects skim coated together can be sanded more quickly than individual defects that are sanded one at a time.

Drywall, the white coat layer of plaster and wood trim surfaces can be skim coated.

DO NOT skim coat surfaces that are wet, water damaged mildewed, mold-affected or in need of repair. These surfaces should be replaced, cleaned, remediated or repaired before surface preparation work begins. *(Refer to Chapter 3)* The skim coating technique is effective only for the filling and concealing of surface damage and cosmetic defects on otherwise sound surfaces.

Note: Skim coating is a combination of both a flush-fill and non-flush repair. For more information on non-flush repairs, and the correct shaping and contouring of applied joint compound over non-flush repairs, *see Chapter 6.*

Figure 5.13
Bathroom wall surface with peeling paint in need of skim coating. The peeling of paint on bathroom ceiling and wall surfaces can often be prevented by using a vent fan while showing or bathing.

Chapter 5 Surface Preparation Techniques

SKIM COATING CEILING AND WALL SURFACES WITH DRYWALL JOINT COMPOUND

Tools and materials

Eye and respiratory system protection, mask, 6" taping knife, putty knife, utility knife, scraper, mud tray and joint compound, fine/medium-grit sanding sponge, wiping cloth or towel, oil-based quick-drying primer/sealer, empty paint can, "all paints" paintbrush, paint thinner and hand cleaner.

Steps

1. Wear eye and respiratory system protection. (*See Pages 19-20 for eye and respiratory system protection information*)

2. Remove peeling paint and any other loose surface material using a putty knife or scraper.

    Use a utility knife to cut any torn pieces of the drywall cover. If the drywall cover has torn edges, or is damaged, refer to REPAIRING DRYWALL COVER DAMAGE, *on Page 152.*

3. Sand the surface with the medium-grit side of a sanding sponge or 80-grit sandpaper. Large areas can be sanded using a pole sander with 80-grit pole sander paper.

    Remove sanding dust with a wiping cloth or towel. Slightly dampening the wiping cloth or towel will help to control dust. Allow any surface moisture to dry before going to *Step 4.*

4. If the surface has drywall cover damage, as shown in *Figure 5.13, on previous page*, seal the edges of the damage and the exposed brown paper (the damaged area) with an oil-based quick drying primer/sealer, or a latex drywall sealer that is capable of sealing down damaged drywall. *(Refer to Figure 6.45, on Page 153)*

    If an oil-based primer/sealer is used, follow application directions in *Step 11*. Allow drying.

5. Partially fill your mud tray with joint compound. A plaster hawk can be used instead of a mud tray to hold joint compound when skim coating large areas.

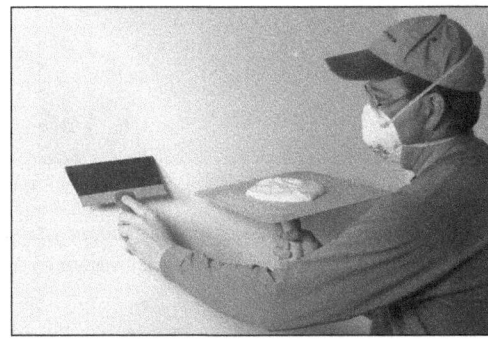

Figure 5.14
A plaster hawk and an 8" or 10" flexible blade taping knife can be used to skim coat larger areas, and entire ceiling and wall surfaces, more quickly than applying drywall joint compound from a mud tray.

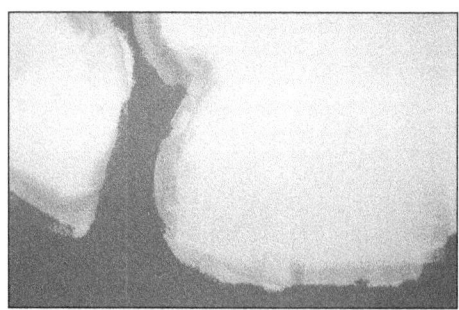

Figure 5.15
Skim coated wall area after two coats of drywall joint compound. Wall area shown is approximately four-feet wide.

Thinness of the joint compound application at the edges illustrates good contouring of the repair. (See Concealing non-flush repairs by applying joint compound with correct shape and contour, on page 110)

Use a putty knife to load a golf ball-sized amount of joint compound onto a 6" taping knife. Slightly larger amounts of joint compound can be used once you feel proficient in your taping knife and skim coating technique. Joint compound should be centered at the end of the blade. *(See Figure 5.4, on Page 63)*

6. Apply a coat of joint compound over areas of damage and/or surface defects. When applying joint compound over large areas, work in sections that are two-feet-square, keeping a wet edge between sections. Allow drying. Joint compound is dry when uniformly white.

7. Sand, or use a putty knife, to remove any rough edges from the first coat of joint compound before applying a second coat. The second coat should make the skim coat uniform, (even in thickness) and the surface smooth. *(Figure 5.15)* Allow drying.

    It is important that the second coat makes the overall skim coat (both coats together) as uniform and smooth as possible. A uniform and smooth skim coat is easier to sand, and is more difficult to detect after priming and painting.

8. Apply a third coat of joint compound if surface damage and/or surface defects are still visible. A third coat will also be needed if the skim coat is not uniform and smooth after the second coat has dried. A partial coat may be sufficient to make the overall skim coat uniform. Spot applications of joint compound may be needed to fill scratches, small holes or uneven areas. Allow drying.

9. Sand skim coated areas with a sanding sponge. *(See How to sand non-flush surface preparation repairs, on Pages 113-114)*

    If you use a pole sander to sand skim coats, use 100-grit or 120-grit pole sander paper. Then do any finish sanding with a sanding sponge.

10. Remove sanding dust with a wiping cloth or towel. Slightly dampening the wiping cloth or towel will help to control dust. Allow any surface moisture to dry before going to *Step 11*.

The removal of sanding dust often exposes areas within the skim coat that are not uniform or smooth. Sand any area that has edges, build-ups or roughness. Apply joint compound to any area that is not uniform, or that was not adequately skim coated. Allow drying, and then re-sand. Remove sanding dust with a wiping cloth or towel.

11. Stir then pour oil-based quick-drying primer/sealer into an empty paint can. Two or three inches in the paint can should be enough to cut in the ceiling or wall surfaces where skim coat repairs have been completed. Apply a coat of oil-based quick-drying primer/sealer over completed repairs. A roller frame, 3/8" nap roller cover, rolling pan and extension rolling pole can be used to apply primer/sealer over large areas or entire ceiling and wall surfaces. Primer/sealer can be applied to smaller areas with a slim roller frame and cover, or a paintbrush. Allow drying.

    Note: If oil-based products are no longer available in your area, use a high-quality latex primer/sealer in this step. Follow directions for cleaning tools, hands and skin. Wear any recommended respiratory system protection.

    Note: If other preparation or repair work will be done, then apply primer/sealer in this room or part of the project after all preparation and repair work has been completed.

12. Lightly sand the dried primer/sealer with the fine-grit side of a sanding sponge. A pole sander with 100-grit or 120-grit pole sander paper may be used in this step to sand large areas.

13. Remove sanding dust with a wiping cloth or towel. Slightly dampening the wiping cloth or towel will help to control dust. Allow any surface moisture to dry before going to *Step 14*.

14. Apply paint, decorative paint, faux finish or stencil.

Refer to Chapter 1 for information regarding safety and avoiding spontaneous combustion fire when using paint thinner, turpentine, mineral spirits, denatured alcohol, paint deglosser, oil-based primers and primer/sealers and White-Pigmented Shellac.

Using a plaster hawk when skim coating

A plaster hawk is a useful tool when skim coating large ceiling and wall surfaces. It enables joint compound to be quickly transferred to the taping knife for application. To start, place a cup or two of joint compound onto the center of the plaster hawk. Place the taping knife blade into the joint compound on the plaster hawk to load the blade for skim coating. Start with a golf ball-sized amount, and then gradually increase the amount of joint compound you load onto the center of the blade. After a few application strokes, use the edge of the plaster hawk to re-center joint compound on the taping knife blade. During skim coating, joint compound will drip off the edges of the blade if it is not re-centered after every few strokes. Re-center joint compound on the taping knife blade using the edge of the plaster hawk. *(Figures 5.16 - 5.19)*

Figure 5.16
Joint compound on taping knife needs to be re-centered.

Figure 5.17
Start by wiping the joint compound onto the edge of the plaster hawk.

Figure 5.18
Load joint compound onto the center of the taping knife blade. If needed, additional joint compound can be loaded onto the taping knife from the plaster hawk.

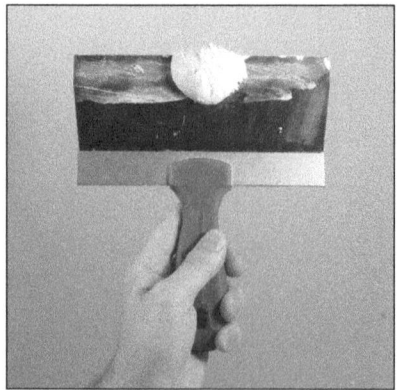

Figure 5.19
Centered joint compound ready for skim coating.

Estimated Time to Complete this Technique

The estimated time to complete the method steps for the skim coating of a surface will vary depending on the size and condition of the surface. Small area skim coats, approximately two-feet square, may require 30-60 minutes of working time, with one or two days needed to complete the repair. Full wall skim coats will require several hours of working time, with two or three days being a realistic goal for completion.

Note: Estimated time to complete method steps includes drying times for repair compounds and primer/sealer. Refer to the directions on the container for drying times of repair compounds and primer/sealer. Humid conditions will lengthen drying times. Other preparation and repair work can be done in the room while waiting for repair compounds to dry.

TIPS AND TROUBLESHOOTING

Skim coating ceiling and wall surfaces

1. Most surface defects can be filled or concealed with two skim coats of drywall joint compound.

   The most common misconception regarding skim coating is that surface defects must be filled or concealed with several heavy (thick) coats of applied joint compound. Thick coats of joint compound add excessive depth to the surface causing needless and arduous sanding. Heavy application can also cause cracks and air bubbles to form in drying joint compound. For best results, apply even, smooth coats of joint compound when skim coating.

2. Keep a "wet edge" when applying joint compound over larger areas.

   Joint compound should be applied in sections approximately two-feet square when skim coating large areas. Large areas may be considered four-feet square, or more. The application of joint compound in two-foot square sections will enable you to keep a wet edge for continuous application over the entire repair surface. Applying joint compound in larger sections may cause the edges to begin drying, resulting in burring and tearing of the joint compound where application sections meet. If necessary, adjust the size of your application section so that you can apply joint compound over the repair surface while maintaining a wet edge.

3. Add water to joint compound if it becomes difficult to apply. Adding water to joint compound will make it easier to apply and give you more working time. Mix a few drops of water into each batch of joint compound in your mud tray or on your plaster hawk. Mix using a paint stirring stick.

Skim coating wood trim surfaces with spackling compound

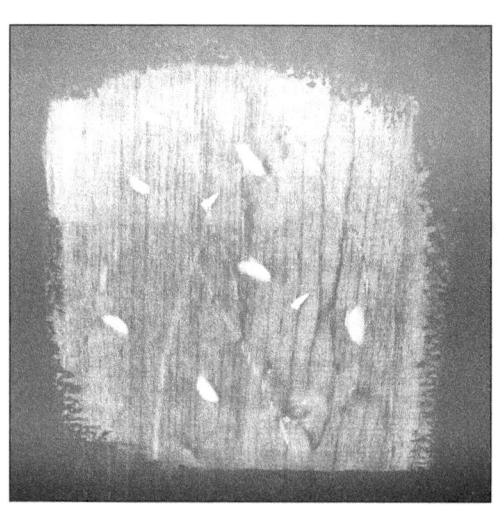

Figure 5.20
Scratches and indentations in wood trim surface are filled by skim coating with spackling compound. Edges of the application have been scraped with a 6" taping knife to eliminate edge build-ups.

Tools and materials

Eye and respiratory system protection, 6" taping knife, putty knife, scraper, mud tray and spackling compound, fine/medium-grit sanding sponge, wiping cloth or towel, oil-based quick-drying primer/sealer, empty paint can, "all paints" paintbrush, paint thinner and hand cleaner.

Steps

1. Wear eye and respiratory system protection.
   (*See Pages 19-20 for eye and respiratory system protection information*)

2. Remove loose material with a putty knife or scraper.

3. Sand the surface with the medium-grit side of a fine/medium sanding sponge or 80-grit sandpaper.

   Indentations and damaged areas should have secure (unraised) edges after scraping and sanding.

4. Remove sanding dust with a wiping cloth or towel. Slightly dampening the wiping cloth or towel will help to control dust. Allow any surface moisture to dry before going to *Step 5*.

5. Use a putty knife to load a workable amount of spackling compound onto the center of the taping knife blade. Start with a small amount.

   A putty knife can be used to apply spackling compound onto small surface areas. And you may find that a putty knife makes application of spackling compound easier on curved trim surfaces.

6. Apply spackling compound over surface defects. On flat surfaces, flush-fill scratches, holes and indentations using the taping knife technique shown in *Diagram 5.1, on Page 61*. On curved surfaces, application strokes should follow the contour of the curve. Remove any excess. Allow drying.

7. Sand, or use a putty knife, to remove any rough edges from the first coat of spackling compound be-

fore applying a second coat. The second coat should make the skim coat uniform and the surface smooth.

Make the second skim coat application as uniform and smooth as possible. Uniform and smooth skim coats *(Fig. 5.20)* are easier to sand than skim coats that are uneven or rough. And a smooth and uniform skim coat is virtually undetectable after careful sanding, priming and painting. Allow drying.

Apply a third coat of spackling compound, if necessary. Allow drying.

8. Lightly sand dried spackling compound with the fine-grit side of a fine/medium sanding sponge. If necessary, the medium-grit side of the sanding sponge can be used to begin sanding, followed by the fine-grit side for finish sanding.

9. Remove sanding dust with a wiping cloth or towel. Slightly dampening the wiping cloth or towel will help to control dust. Allow any surface moisture to dry before going to *Step 10*.

   The removal of sanding dust often exposes areas within the skim coat that are not smooth or uniform. Sand any area that has build-ups or roughness. The surface should be smooth after sanding. Apply spackling compound to any area that was not adequately skim coated. Allow drying, and then sand. After sanding, remove sanding dust with a wiping cloth or towel.

10. Stir then pour oil-based quick-drying primer/sealer into an empty paint can. An inch or two in the paint can will usually be enough to prime the filled holes, indentations and scratches in the wood trim in several rooms. Apply a coat of oil-based quick-drying primer/sealer over completed repairs. Primer/sealer can be applied to trim areas with a paintbrush. A slim roller frame and cover can be used for larger areas. Allow drying.

    Note: If oil-based products are no longer available in your area, use a high-quality latex primer/sealer in this step. Follow directions for cleaning tools, hands and skin. Wear any recommended respiratory system protection.

    Note: If other preparation or repair work will be done, then apply primer/sealer in this room or part of the project after all preparation and repair work has been completed.

11. Lightly sand the dried primer/sealer with the fine-grit side of a sanding sponge or fine-grit sandpaper.

    Remove sanding dust with a wiping cloth or towel. Slightly dampening the wiping cloth or towel will help to control dust. Allow any surface moisture to dry before going to *Step 12*.

12. Apply paint, decorative paint, faux finish or stencil.

Refer to Chapter 1 for information regarding safety and avoiding spontaneous combustion fire when using paint thinner, turpentine, mineral spirits, denatured alcohol, paint deglosser, oil-based primers and primer/sealers and White-Pigmented Shellac.

Estimated Time to Complete this Technique

The estimated time to complete the method steps for the skim coating of a wood surface will vary depending on the size and condition of the surface. The skim coating of a windowsill may require four hours to complete, with an actual working time of approximately thirty minutes.

Note: Estimated time to complete steps includes drying times for repair compounds and primer/sealer. Refer to the directions on the container for drying times of repair compounds and primer/sealer. Humid conditions will lengthen drying times. Other preparation and repair work can be done in the room while waiting for repair compounds to dry.

TIPS AND TROUBLESHOOTING

Skim coating wood surfaces

1. Follow the directions for thinning should spackling compound become difficult to apply.

2. Avoid excessive application of spackling compound. Coats that are too thick may crack during drying.

3. Deep holes and indentations should be filled using wood filler. (*See* REPAIRING HOLES AND INDENTATIONS IN WOOD SURFACES WITH WOOD FILLER, *on Page 120)*

Note: Damaged wood trim surfaces may need to be replaced.

Using painter's putty to fill nail sets and miter gaps on wood surfaces

Painter's putty is used on wood trim surfaces to fill nail set holes and nail-sized holes. It can also be used to fill small gaps between mitered pieces of trim wood. Painter's putty can be applied using a putty knife, or by hand.

Tools and materials

Eye and respiratory system protection, painter's putty, putty knife, scraper, fine/medium-grit sanding sponge or 80-grit sandpaper, duster, wiping cloth and hand cleaner.

Steps

1. Wear eye and respiratory system protection.
   (See Pages 19-20 for eye and respiratory system protection information)

2. Use a putty knife or scraper to remove any loose material and peeling paint from the surface bordering the hole or gap you will fill with painter's putty.

3. Sand the surface bordering the hole or gap with the medium-grit side of a sanding sponge or 80-grit sandpaper.

4. Remove sanding dust with a wiping cloth or towel. Slightly dampening the wiping cloth or towel will help to control dust. Allow any surface moisture to dry before going to *Step 5*.

5. Roll a marble-sized amount of painter's putty between your hands for about thirty seconds. Rolling warms painter's putty making it easier to apply.

6. Use a putty knife or fingers to apply painter's putty to fill nail sets, nail-sized holes or the gaps between mitered pieces of wood. Painter's putty should be applied flush to the surface with no excess outside the hole or gap. *(Figure 5.22)*

7. Allow drying as per instructions on the painter's putty can.

Figure 5.21
Nail set hole in baseboard.

Figure 5.22
Nail set hole filled with painter's putty.

8. After drying, prime surfaces as per instructions on the can. When applying priming product, wear any recommended respiratory system protection. Primed surfaces should be lightly sanded when dry.

9. Remove sanding dust with a wiping cloth or towel. Slightly dampening the wiping cloth or towel will help to control dust. Allow any surface moisture to dry before going to *Step 10*.

10. Apply paint, decorative paint, faux finish or stencil.

Refer to Chapter 1 for information regarding safety and avoiding spontaneous combustion fire when using paint thinner, turpentine, mineral spirits, denatured alcohol, paint deglosser, oil-based primers and primer/sealers and White-Pigmented Shellac.

Estimated Time to Complete this Technique

The estimated time to complete the filling of nail sets, nail-sized holes and the gaps between mitered pieces of trim wood is one minute per fill.

TIPS AND TROUBLESHOOTING

***Using painter's putty to fill nail sets
and miter gaps on wood surfaces***

1. Apply painter's putty to flush-fill the hole or gap. **Do NOT** apply beyond the hole or gap.

2. Painter's putty should not be used on ceiling or wall surfaces.

3. Larger holes in wood surfaces should be filled using either spackling compound or wood filler.
   (See APPLICATION OF SPACKLING COMPOUND, on Page 72)
   (See REPAIRING HOLES AND INDENTATIONS IN WOOD SURFACES WITH WOOD FILLER, on Page 120)

   Note: Trim surfaces with a large hole or miter gap may need to be replaced.

Sanding

Why sanding is important

Sanding promotes the durable adhesion of repair compounds, primers and paint-especially on surfaces coated with a glossed finish paint. It also provides an aesthetic dividend by helping to make surfaces smoother and more uniform. And careful sanding of flush-fills and repairs helps to make fills and repairs virtually undetectable after priming and painting.

Note: Gloss paint finishes include: Matte, Low-luster, Eggshell, Semi-gloss and Full-gloss.

Alternatives to manual sanding

With the implementation of the EPA's Renovate, Repair and Painting rule (RRP), attention is being focused on the containment of sanding and construction-related dust that may contain lead. In response to the dangers of lead dust, homeowners preparing surfaces in homes built before 1978 should consider using "dustless" sanding techniques and products during the course of surface preparation. If your house was built before 1978, "dustless" sanding techniques should be used if children and/or pets live, or are regularly present, in the house. Even if your house was built in 1978, or later, it may still be wise to use "dustless" sanding techniques if children and/or pets live, or are regularly present, in the house. If your house was built before 1978, talk with your paint dealer about "dustless" sanding techniques and products that will help you to reduce, or eliminate, the need for manual sanding.

(See: Be informed as to the hazards of lead, on Page 16)
(See Protecting children and Protecting pets, on Page 23)
(See: Dustless sanding, on Pages 92-93)

Before sanding surfaces, read the information about lead on Pages 16-17.

Always wear eye and respiratory system protection when sanding. Information about eye and respiratory system protection can be found on Pages 19-20.

If you use an electric sander to sand painted surfaces, be sure that your sander is equipped with a HEPA Filter attachment.

A HEPA vacuum is more efficient (offers greater protection) than a regular vacuum cleaner when vacuuming sanding or construction-related dust that may contain lead.

Chapter 5 Surface Preparation Techniques

Surface Prep Tip

Remove flecks before sanding

Flecks are small surface particles. They often consist of crumb-sized pieces of dried paint film, repair compound and sanding dust that have become part of the painted surface. Surface sanding does not always remove flecks, especially larger flecks. Remove flecks from painted surfaces by gently scraping them using a rigid blade putty knife, or scraper. Once flecks have been removed, sand ceiling, wall and trim surfaces.

If fleck removal leaves a surface indentation, fill with joint compound using the *Taping knife technique for flush-fills shown in Diagram 5.1, on Page 61.*

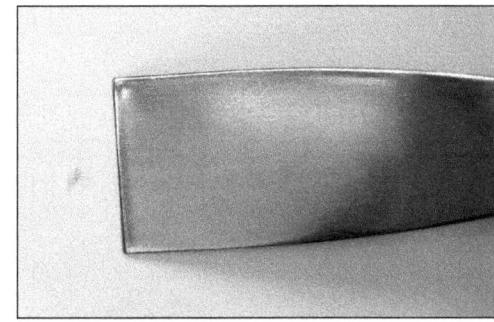
Figure 5.23
Surface fleck.

Preventing flecks

Surface flecks can be prevented by following these tips:

1. After sanding repairs on ceiling and wall surfaces, remove sanding dust with a wiping cloth or towel. Use a duster to remove sanding dust from sanded wood trim.
2. Strain stored primers and paint before application.
3. Thoroughly clean paintbrushes after use to remove dried paint on bristles.
4. Thoroughly clean empty paint cans, rolling frames, rolling pans and rolling screens after use.

Surface Prep Tip

Use worn sanding tools for extra-smooth surface sanding

Keep a collection of worn sandpaper and sanding sponges for fine and extra-smooth finish sanding. Worn sanding tools also enable very small amounts of repair compound to be removed from flush-fills and repairs, helping to create completed flush-fills and repairs that are virtually undetectable.

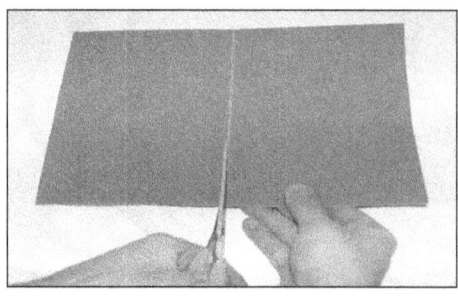

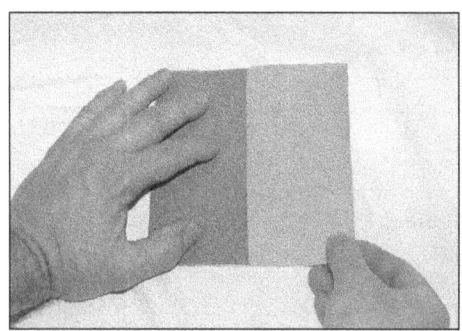

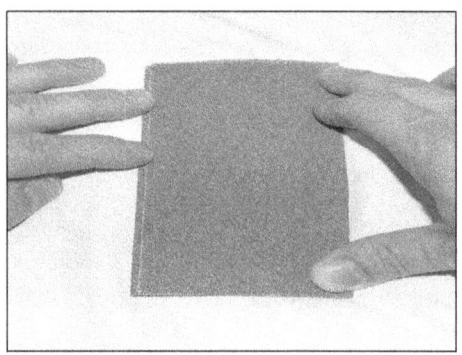

Figures 5.24, 5.25, 5.26
Folding sandpaper. Using this method gives you three sanding surfaces.

Sanding tools

A variety of sanding tools are available to help you sand ceiling, wall and trim surfaces. Each tool has unique characteristics that you can utilize for the sanding needs of your project. In this section, three common sanding tools are covered.

Sandpaper

Sandpaper can be used on ceiling, wall and trim surfaces. Ceiling and wall surfaces can be spot sanded with sandpaper to remove small flecks. On wood trim surfaces, sandpaper is used to dull the finish of the existing paint before new paint is applied. Always sand in the direction of the wood grain and use care to avoid damaging any edges or details of the wood trim.

Avoid using sandpaper to sand flush-fills and repairs completed with drywall joint compound, as pressure applied by fingers can cause wavy lines or grooves in sanded fills and repairs.

The sandpaper grit number helps you to choose the right sandpaper for each sanding task. The lower the grit number the coarser the sanding grit is on the sandpaper; the higher the grit number the finer the grit material is on the sandpaper. Begin sanding rough surfaces with 50- or 60-grit sandpaper. Once surface roughness is removed, use either 80-grit or 100-grit sandpaper for smooth finish sanding. For extra-smooth surface sanding on wood trim surfaces, finish sand with a 120- or 150-grit sandpaper.

Latex surface sandpaper

Wood trim painted with a latex (water-based) paint may become gummy, pill or tear when sanded. Gloss-finish latex paints are much more prone to these sanding problems than flat-finish latex paints.

Latex surface sandpaper prevents much of the gumminess and tearing that can occur when latex-painted surfaces are sanded with regular sandpaper. Try using a latex surface sandpaper on your trim if you experience any of the sanding problems listed above.

Folding sandpaper

Fold a sheet of sandpaper in-half from top-to-bottom. Then use scissors to cut along the fold. Fold each half-sheet into thirds. Each folded piece of sandpaper has three sanding surfaces that can be rotated when fresh sandpaper is needed. *(Figures 5.24 - 5.26)*

Sanding sponge

The sanding sponge is ideal for sanding flush-fills, and repairs completed with drywall joint compound, lightweight spackling compound and spackling compound. Small holes, indentations and scratches filled with wood filler can also be sanded using a sanding sponge. On fills and repairs completed with joint compound, the block shape of the sanding sponge eliminates finger grooves and waviness that can occur when joint compound is hand-sanded using sandpaper. Sanding sponges are available in grit levels from fine to coarse, and in a varying sizes. *(Figures 5.27 and 5.28)*

For more on the sanding sponge, see *Why a sanding sponge should be used to sand non-flush repairs, on Page 113*.

Pole sander

The pole sander is used to sand ceiling and wall surfaces. Its long handle and swivel-base sanding platform enable large areas, or entire ceiling and wall surfaces, to be sanded quickly. Pole sander paper is fastened onto the sanding platform with screw clamps. 80-grit pole sander paper can be used with the pole sander to sand most ceiling and wall surfaces. 100-grit or 120-grit pole sander paper can be used to sand smooth surfaces, and for finish sanding. *(Figure 5.29)*

When sanding newly-installed, finished drywall, professional drywall finishers will often use a pole sander, or vacuum-enabled sanding machine with a sanding platform similar to the pole sander's, to quickly do the bulk of the sanding work. Most pros will then use large "drywall finishing" sanding sponges to detail-sand any remaining edges or imperfections.

Note: When a pole sander has been used to sand the drywall joint compound on a new drywall surface, finish sand with the fine-grit side of a sanding sponge. With a sanding sponge, you will be able to sand out any small surface imperfections that may be missed by pole sanding.

Figures 5.27 and 5.28
Sanding sponge.

Figure 5.29
Wall sanding with a pole sander.

In homes built before 1978, it may be wise to avoid pole sanding, or any other method of entire ceiling or wall surface sanding, due to the possibility of creating sanding dust which may contain lead. *(See Dustless sanding, on Page 92)*

Dustless sanding

Sanding dust can be harmful to breathe, and if your house was constructed before 1978, the sanding of painted surfaces can cause the airborne spread of lead-containing dust. To obtain an extra measure of safety in homes constructed before 1978, "dustless" sanding techniques can be used.

"Dustless" sanding techniques create considerably less dust than surface sanding done with traditional abrasives, such as sandpaper. If your house was built before 1978, be sure to discuss the use of "dustless" sanding techniques and products with your paint dealer.

Dustless sanding techniques

Wet sanding with a damp cloth or sponge

A damp wiping cloth or sponge can be used to "wet" sand surface preparation fills and repairs. Lightly apply the dampened wiping cloth or sponge to the fill or repair using a sanding motion. A damp wiping cloth can be wrapped around a sanding sponge to create a "wet sanding block." Go over the surface several times with light pressure to remove small amounts of the dried repair compound. Excessive pressure often results in removal of too much repair compound. Allow drying. Repeat as necessary until the fill or repair appears to blend with the surface. If too much repair compound was removed, reapply and wet sand after drying. Allow thorough drying of all wet-sanded fills and repairs before the application of primer or primer/sealer.

Note: Spackling compound must be fully cured before wet sanding. As the directions for drying pertain to manual sanding time and not wet sanding time, contact the manufacturer and ask them for the time required for their spackling compound to fully cure before wet sanding.

Note: DO NOT attempt to wet sand wood filler.

Chemical "sanding" with a paint deglosser

The application of a paint deglosser softens the gloss finish of paint on trim wood preparing it for painting without the need for manual surface sanding. Some deglossers also clean the surface.

Paint deglossers are not necessary on flat-finish-painted surfaces.

Using a primer or primer/sealer that can bond to painted surfaces without first sanding

Another method that can be used to avoid manual sanding is the application of a primer or primer/sealer that is capable of bonding to a gloss-finish-painted surface that has not been sanded or wiped with a chemical paint deglosser. This technique is especially effective for application over gloss-finish-painted ceiling, wall and trim surfaces that would otherwise need to be surface-sanded, or "scuffed," with sandpaper to promote surface adhesion (bonding) with applied paint.

In many cases, flat-finish-painted ceiling and wall surfaces do not need to be either surface-sanded or coated with primer or primer/sealer (when stain-free) to achieve a durable bond with applied paint.

Using paint remover

Paint removing products provide another alternative that can reduce the need for manual sanding when removing multiple layers of paint from wood trim surfaces. *(See Surface Prep Tip, on next page)*

Note: If you are unsure of the surface preparation or sanding requirements of any surface, consult with your paint dealer.

Chapter 5 Surface Preparation Techniques

 **Surface Prep Tip**

Removing multiple layers of paint from wood surfaces

Sanding is not always an efficient or safe way to remove multiple layers of paint from wood surfaces. Attempting to remove multiple layers of paint by sanding can be time consuming and damaging to wood surfaces. And the dust made airborne by sanding multiple layers of paint can be harmful to breathe.

Using a blowtorch or heat gun to remove paint from surfaces can cause fire. Heating paint before removal may also cause fumes that are harmful to breathe.

Multiple layers of paint can be removed from wood surfaces with paint remover. Ask your paint dealer to recommend a paint-removing product for your surface preparation project. Read and follow the directions for use and safety precautions. Wear eye, hand and respiratory system protection during use.

When using a paint deglosser or paint removing product, follow all manufacturer's directions for use and safety guidelines. Wear chemical-resistant rubber gloves, eye and respiratory system protection, and apply only in rooms and areas with adequate ventilation. Do NOT apply in a closed or sealed room or area. *(See Chapter 1 for safety information, including* AVOIDING SPONTANEOUS COMBUSTION FIRE, *on Page 24)*

Estimated Time to Complete this Technique

The estimated time to complete the sanding tasks in a room will often range between fifteen and sixty minutes. Small rooms often require less than a half-hour of sanding. Larger rooms, and rooms with extensive repair work or wood trim, may require more than one hour to sand.

TIPS AND TROUBLESHOOTING

Sanding

1. The best tip for sanding repairs is the correct application of repair compounds. Correctly applied repair compounds create a repair that requires minimal sanding.

2. On wood surfaces, sand in the direction of the wood grain.

3. Sand gloss paint finishes until the gloss has been dulled. Wood trim surfaces finished with polyurethane (that will be primed and painted) should also be sanded until the polyurethane finish has been dulled.
   Note: Gloss paint finishes include: Matte, Low-luster, Eggshell, Semi-gloss and Full-gloss.

4. Use a sanding sponge instead of folded sandpaper to sand completed joint compound repairs. The block shape of the sanding sponge eliminates finger groove marks that can occur when hand sanding joint compound repairs with folded, or unfolded, sandpaper.

5. Pole sanding ceiling and wall surfaces helps to remove small flecks. *(See Figure 5.23, on Page 89)*

6. The edges, or borders, of repairs should be sanded until they are "feathered" into the surrounding surface. A feathered surface, or edge, will gradually raise or lower until it meets the surrounding surface. The gradual slope of a feathered edge will help the eye to see a smooth and uniform surface, concealing the repair. Abrupt edges, or slopes, attract the eye's attention, revealing the repair.

7. Removing sanding dust from sanded surfaces and repairs with a wiping cloth or towel helps to reveal any areas of the repair that need additional repair compound application or sanding. It also helps to prevent sanding dust from forming flecks during priming and painting.

8. If your home was constructed before 1978, talk with your paint dealer about "dustless" sanding techniques and products.

CAULKING

Caulk is used to fill gaps. Apply caulk to fill any gaps between wall surfaces and wood trim. It can also be applied to fill the gap between joined pieces of wood trim. Caulking provides an immediate aesthetic dividend, as well-caulked surfaces have a uniform and finished appearance that is pleasing to the eye. Gaps and joints left without caulk are easily detectable and detract from an otherwise good paint job, decorative finish, faux finish, mural or stencil application.

Apply a paintable latex caulk to fill the gaps between painted wall surfaces and painted wood trim. *(See Note at bottom of page)* Joints between new (bare) wood trim and wall surfaces should also be caulked. Gaps and joints should be filled with caulk so that the entire join, or joint, looks uniform. Good caulk application makes surfaces look as if they join together perfectly without caulk.

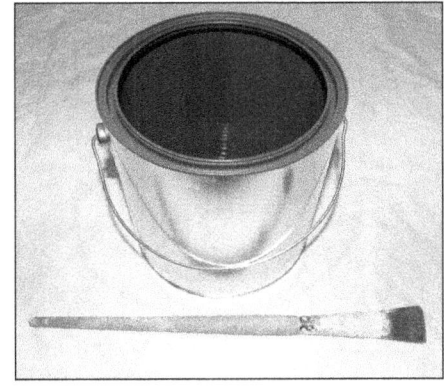

Figure 5.30
Empty one-gallon paint can and Fitch brush.

Gaps and joints that may need caulk can often be found along baseboards *(Fig. 5.37, on Page 97)*, chair railing, door moldings, window moldings and mantles. Along baseboards, caulk any gap between the baseboard and wall surface. Also caulk the gap or joint between a painted quarter-round or shoe molding, and a painted baseboard. Small gaps where baseboards, quarter-rounds or shoe moldings meet in corners should also be caulked. *(Larger gaps should be filled with painter's putty, See Page 85)* Caulk any gap or joint between wall surfaces and the top of the chair railing. Small gaps where chair rail meets in corners should also be caulked (larger gaps should be filled with painter's putty). The gap or joint between door and window frames and their trim molding, called a "reveal" *(a reveal can be seen in Figures 5.38 and 5.40)*, should also be caulked. Caulk the gap or joint where the door trim molding and baseboard meet, and the gap or joint between a door frame and door stop. *(Fig. 5.40, on Page 97)* Also caulk the gap or joint between the wall surface and a mantle.

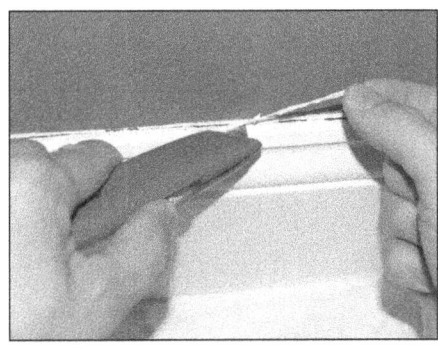

Figure 5.31
Remove any loose caulk before applying new caulk. Also remove all caulk where the caulk joint has split. *(as seen in photo above)* Use a utility knife to gently remove caulk from both the wall and trim surfaces.

Note: Split caulk joints may indicate the need to fasten trim closer to the surface with finishing nails.

Small gaps that may need to be caulked can often be found between mitered corner pieces of painted wood trim, such as in wainscoting, door moldings *(Fig. 5.38, on Page 97)*, window moldings, chair railing and baseboards. Large gaps should be filled with painter's putty. *(See USING PAINTER'S PUTTY TO FILL NAIL SETS AND MITER GAPS ON WOOD SURFACES, on Page 85)*

Paintable latex adhesive caulk should be applied to fill the gap or joint between ceiling and wall surfaces and crown molding, and the small corner miter gaps in crown molding. An adhesive caulk has more bonding strength than a regular caulk, which helps to prevent crown molding from separating or gapping from ceiling and wall surfaces.

Note: Avoid caulking the gaps in stained, varnished or polyurethane-finished surfaces. Also refrain from caulking the gaps between ceiling or wall surfaces and stained, varnished or polyurethane-finished surfaces. Avoid caulking the gap between a painted baseboard and a stained shoe mold, or quarter-round.

The Homeowner's Guide to Surface Preparation for Interior House Painting

Figure 5.32
Make an angle cut on your new tube of caulk.

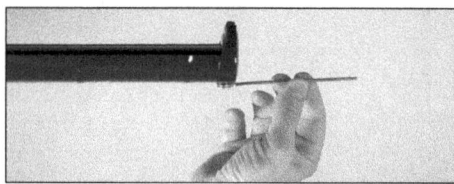

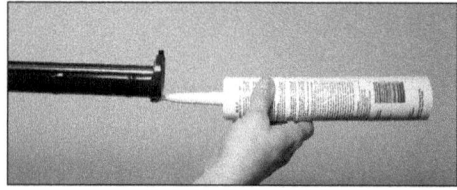

Figures 5.33, 5.34
Breaking the seal with the puncture rod.

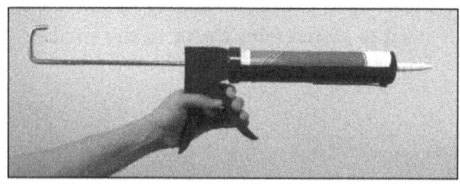

Figure 5.35
Caulk tube installed into caulk gun. You are ready for caulking.

Figure 5.36
Turning plunger handle to stop caulk flow. You will hear a click and feel the pressure release as the caulk flow stops.

Tools and materials

Eye and respiratory system protection, caulking gun, paintable latex or latex adhesive caulk, putty knife, utility knife, 80-grit sandpaper, measuring tape or ruler, pen, 3/4" or 1" round latex bristle "Fitch" brush *(Fig. 5.30, on Page 95)*, empty paint can with one inch of water, wiping cloth.

Steps

1. Wear eye and respiratory system protection. (*See Pages 19-20 for eye and respiratory system protection information*)

2. Remove any loosened caulk. *(Fig. 5.31, on Page 95)* A utility knife can be used to carefully cut lengths of loosened caulk before removal. Sand the surface after caulk removal.

3. Remove debris with a duster, and then wipe the surface with a wiping cloth or towel. Slightly dampening the wiping cloth or towel will help to control dust. Allow any surface moisture to dry before going to *Step 4*.

4. Measure, mark and cut the caulk tube nozzle at a 45-degree angle 1/4" from the tip. This angled cut will produce a small stream of caulk called a "bead." A small bead is easy to apply and control. The cut should end just before the tip. *(Fig 5.32)*

5. Use the seal puncture rod on the bottom of the caulk gun or a straightened hanger to break the seal on the caulk tube. The seal is at the bottom of the nozzle. *(Figs. 5.33 and 5.34)* Wipe rod and replace under caulk gun after puncturing seal.

6. Install caulk tube into caulk gun. *(Fig. 5.35)*

7. To apply caulk, hold the caulk gun at approximately a 45-degree angle to the surface. With the angle-cut tip of the caulk tube placed into or on top of the gap or joint, gently squeeze the trigger handle and move the caulk gun along the length of the gap or joint. Use even pressure on the trigger handle to apply a thin, even bead to fill the gap or joint. *(Figs. 5.37 and 5.38, opposite page)* Avoid caulk application outside of the gap or joint. Remove the caulk gun from the surface and turn the plunger handle one-half turn to release pressure on the caulk tube stopping caulk flow. *(Fig. 5.36)*

8. Dip the Fitch brush into the paint can. Tap off excess water. The Fitch should not be dripping when it is removed from the can. Use the wet Fitch to brush the caulk bead into the gap or joint. Re-dip the Fitch as needed to wet-brush the entire bead of caulk smoothly and uniformly into place. Smooth any caulk build-ups or heavy edges. If necessary, remove excess applied caulk with a wiping cloth. Re-apply caulk to any areas that were not uniformly filled. Wet-brush until the bead is smooth and uniform. Use light, long strokes to complete the wet-brushing process. *(Figs. 5.39 and 5.40)*

9. Remove any water from wall and trim surfaces with a clean wiping cloth. Do not touch wet-brushed caulk with the wiping cloth. *(Figure 5.41, on Page 98)*

10. Continue to caulk and wet-brush in small sections until caulking work is complete. Try working larger sections after mastering smaller ones. For best results, allow caulking to dry for several hours, or overnight. Painting or priming wet caulk is not recommended, as brush bristles often ruin the smooth finish of applied caulk.

11. Re-caulk any gaps that are visible after the first application of caulk has dried. Wet-brush to smooth, then allow drying. Large applications of caulk can affect the finish of applied paint. Any area that requires a second application of caulking should be sealed with one coat of oil-based quick dry primer/sealer after the second application of caulk has dried. Primer/sealer prevents large areas of dried caulk from "shining" through applied paint.

    Note: If oil-based products are no longer available in your area, use a high-quality latex primer/sealer capable of priming and sealing caulk in this step. Follow directions for cleaning tools, hands and skin. Wear recommended respiratory system protection.

12. Apply paint, decorative paint, faux finish or stencil.

Refer to Chapter 1 for information regarding safety and avoiding spontaneous combustion fire when using paint thinner, turpentine, mineral spirits, denatured alcohol, paint deglosser, oil-based primers and primer/sealers and White-Pigmented Shellac.

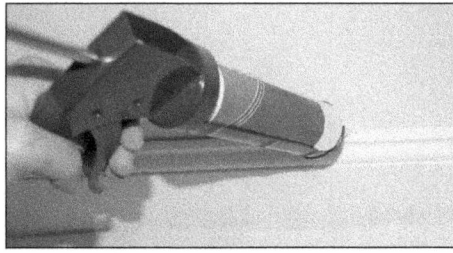

Figure 5.37
Applying a thin bead of caulk between wall and baseboard.

Figure 5.38
Caulk can be used to fill small gaps in mitered wood trim moldings.

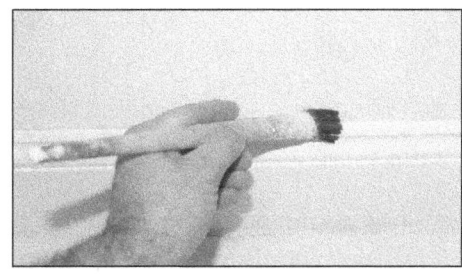

Figures 5.39, 5.40
Wet-brushing caulk along baseboard (top), door stop trim (bottom).

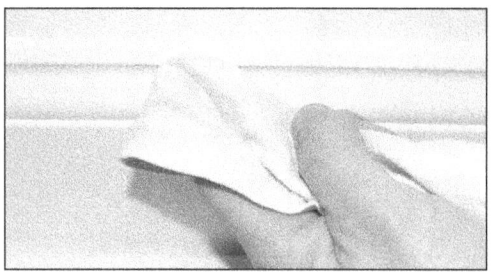

Figure 5.41
Remove excess water with a clean wiping cloth. Be careful not to touch wet-brushed caulk.

Estimated Time to Complete this Technique

The actual time applying and wet brushing caulk in one room will often range between fifteen and sixty minutes. Removing loose caulk from surfaces during preparation will extend the working time needed to complete this technique.

TIPS AND TROUBLESHOOTING

Caulking

1. Cut the nozzle correctly for proper caulk bead size. *(Step 4)* The most common caulking problem is excessive caulk application. This is often the result of a caulk tube nozzle opening that is too large. Excessive caulk application is difficult to wet-brush to a uniform consistency.

2. Apply small beads of caulk. *(Step 7)* You often need less caulk than you may think to fill a gap. Apply a small bead of caulk to fill the gap, and then wet-brush to a uniform consistency. When dry, apply a second small bead of caulk if, necessary. Small beads are easier to control and require much less wet-brushing. Avoid rounded applications of caulk. Proper caulk application makes the surface and wood trim, or the joints of wood trim, appear as if it were almost perfectly joined without any caulk.

3. After wet-brushing caulk, wipe excess water from the surface to avoid the formation of caulk film. *(Step 9, Figure 5.41)* Water used during wet-brush caulking picks up small amounts of caulk that leaves a white film deposit when dry. Wherever the water has

dripped or settled, you will likely see caulk film. Dried caulk film can often be removed by wiping with a moistened wiping cloth. If dried caulk film can not be removed by wiping, then remove it by sanding with 80-grit sandpaper.

4. Gaps of 1/8" or more between wood trim and ceiling and wall surfaces should not be caulked until the wood trim is nailed closer to the ceiling or wall surface, when possible. Try to close the gap by nailing, but do not use excessive force to "bend" trim or molding into place. Excessive force can cause the trim or molding to split. Apply caulk after the trim or molding is as close as it can be to ceiling or wall surfaces. Larger gaps will require an addition application of caulk. Large fills of caulk should receive one coat of oil-based quick-drying primer/sealer after the caulk has dried.

5. Consider replacing any trim or molding with a miter gap of ¼" or greater.

6. A miter gap of less than 1/16" in painted door casing or window trim can be filled with caulk. Gaps of 1/16" or more should be filled with painter's putty.

7. A gap of less than 1/16" in the joined pieces of wood, such as in a door, can be filled with caulk or painter's putty. Gaps between 1/16"- 1/8" should be filled with painter's putty. Larger gaps may indicate a problem with the door that requires repair or replacement by a licensed professional carpenter.

8. Caulk the gap between the top of door or window trim molding and the wall when the top of door or window trim molding is visible from a stairway or the second floor. Paint the top of all caulked trim molding as you would the rest of the trim.

Priming and sealing

This section presents general information about primer, primer/sealer, underbody primer and White-Pigmented Shellac. Ask your paint dealer for the best priming and sealing products to complete the specific priming and sealing tasks of your interior surface preparation project.

Types of primers and sealers

Primer

Primer adheres durably to a variety of substrates. It bonds successfully where paint alone may fail. Primer also helps to fill, or "surface seal," absorbent areas on surfaces, allowing paint to spread evenly and dry uniformly. Uniform drying is essential for a consistent finish when applying glossed paint.
Note: Gloss paint finishes include: Matte, Low-luster, Eggshell, Semi-gloss and Full-gloss.

Primer/sealer

Primer/sealers combine the qualities of durable adhesion (surface bonding), surface sealing and stain sealing, and some primer/sealers can also be used as a "barrier coat" between layers (substrates) of latex and oil-based paints. A barrier coat is necessary to prevent oil-based and latex paint substrates from meeting, which could cause poor paint adhesion (lack of durable bonding between the substrates) resulting in areas of peeling paint. Before applying a latex paint over a surface previously painted with an oil-based paint (or vice-versa), first apply a primer/sealer that can act as a barrier between layers of oil-based and latex paints.

Oil-based primer/sealers, at the time of the writing of this book, still offer a higher level of stain-sealing ability than latex primer/sealers.

Underbody or Undercoater

Underbody primers, also called "undercoaters," can be used to prime new (bare) wood and previously-painted wood trim before the application of paint. Underbody primers are often thicker than other primers and dry more slowly. The slower drying process of underbody primers allows for greater primer surface penetration. It also helps to reduce, or "level," paintbrush bristle marks. When properly applied, underbody primer has a smooth, uniform appearance with a minimum of visible brush marks when dry. Wood trim has a richer look when paint is applied over an underbody primer. Some underbody and undercoater primers have stain sealing ability. Underbody and undercoater primers are available that can be used as a "barrier coat" between layers (substrates) of latex and oil-based paints.

White-Pigmented Shellac

White-Pigmented Shellac is used to seal the toughest stains, such as wood knots, wood tannin and severe water staining. Use White-Pigmented Shellac to seal wood knots, wood tannin, severe water staining and any stains that bleed though primer/sealer. Several coats may be needed to seal knots and stains. Follow manufacturer's directions for drying times and re-coating.

Priming and sealing situations

New or repaired plaster

New plaster, and areas of plaster repaired by a plasterer, should be primed and sealed with an oil-based primer/sealer after curing. (Be sure to ask the plasterer for the curing time of completed repairs) Lightly sand dried primer/sealer with the fine-grit side of a sanding sponge. A pole sander with 100-grit or 120-grit pole sander paper can be used to sand large areas. Remove sanding dust with a wiping cloth or towel, and then apply paint, decorative paint, faux finish or stencils.

> **Note:** If oil-based products are no longer available in your area, use a high-quality latex primer/sealer capable of priming and sealing new plaster.

Painted plaster surfaces

Completed surface preparation repairs on the white coat layer of the plaster surface should be primed and sealed with an oil-based quick-drying primer/sealer, or latex primer/sealer capable of priming and sealing plaster surfaces.

After the removal of wallpaper and borders

Use an oil-based quick-drying primer/sealer to seal surfaces after wallpaper and border removal.

> #### *Why primer/sealer is needed on surfaces after wallpaper and border removal*
>
> A coat of oil-based quick-drying primer/sealer is needed after wallpaper and/or border removal as wallpaper paste often gets absorbed into wall surfaces. (and ceiling surfaces where wallpaper was applied) Wallpaper paste removal cleaning removes surface paste, but may not remove absorbed paste. Within the absorbed paste, material is present that can cause staining upon contact with the moisture from applied paint. The mixing of absorbed paste and moisture from applied paint can cause a rusty-colored cloudiness, or areas of solid color staining in the applied paint. The application of one coat of oil-based quick-drying primer/sealer, after cleaning wallpaper paste residue and completing all surface preparation techniques and repairs, seals the surface and prevents any absorbed paste from mixing with newly applied paint. In cases where wallpaper or border removal has caused drywall cover damage, a coat of oil-based quick-drying primer/sealer should be applied after surfaces are cleaned and have dried. (See Repairing drywall cover damage, on Page 152)

> **Note:** If oil-based products are no longer available in your area, use a high-quality latex primer/sealer capable of sealing previously wallpapered surfaces.

After cleaning soiled surfaces

Apply a coat of oil-based primer/sealer to the surface (when dry) if any visible soiling or stain residue remains after repeated cleaning. To prevent bleed through of soiling or staining material that may have been absorbed into the surface, a coat of oil-based quick-drying primer/sealer should be applied to surfaces that were cleaned due to heavy soiling, nicotine stain, food stain, ballpoint pen (or other ink writing instrument), smoke, soot and surface marks. (even if surfaces appear clean after cleaning)

Note: If oil-based products are no longer available in your area, use a high-quality latex primer/sealer capable of priming and sealing surfaces with stains and soiling.

On surfaces repaired with drywall joint compound, or other repair compounds

Surfaces repaired with joint compound, or other repair compounds, should be primed and sealed with an oil-based primer/sealer. Oil-based quick-drying primer/sealer helps to prevent the bubbling (blistering) of applied paint over areas repaired with joint compound and other repair compounds. It also seals the alkyd resin found in some spackling compounds preventing them from causing visible surface variations, such as shinny or dull areas in the finish of painted surfaces.

For best results, avoid spot priming and apply a full coat of oil-based quick-drying primer/sealer on ceiling and wall surfaces where repair work has been completed. A full coat of primer/sealer will provide a uniform substrate that will help to prevent the possibility of visible paint finish variations that can occur when paint is applied on a surface comprised of differing substrates.

Note: If oil-based products are no longer available in your area, use a high-quality latex primer/sealer capable of priming and sealing surfaces after repair with the repair compound, or compounds, that you have used.

Before the application of decorative paint, faux finish, mural art and stencils

Painted plaster and drywall surfaces should be primed and sealed with an oil-based quick-drying primer/sealer after surface preparation. For best results, avoid spot priming and apply a full coat of oil-based quick-drying primer/sealer to ceiling and wall surfaces where repair work has been completed. A full coat of primer/sealer will provide a uniform substrate that will help to prevent visible surface variations in the finish of the decorative paint, faux finish, mural art or stencil paint that can occur when the surface is spot primed. From a surface preparation standpoint, oil-based primer/sealer is a better choice than latex primer/sealer when working with decorative paint, faux finish, mural and stencil paint because it provides more surface sealing than latex primer/sealer. The additional surface sealing properties of oil-based primer/sealer provide more working time for decorative paint, faux finish, mural art and stencil paint. That being said, *ask the decorative paint, faux finish, mural art paint or stencil paint manufacturer's representative to recommend the best primer/sealer for the surface conditions in which you will be applying their materials.*

After surface preparation and sanding, remove sanding dust with a wiping cloth or towel, and then apply primer/sealer. (or recommended priming and sealing product) Allow drying, then lightly sand using a pole sander with 100-grit or 120-grit pole sander paper. Remove sanding dust with a wiping cloth or towel, and then apply decorative paint, faux finish, mural paint or stencil paint.

New drywall

New drywall should be primed and sealed with either an oil-based or latex primer/sealer. Primer/sealers provide new drywall a level of surface sealing that enables applied paint to spread evenly, and paint finishes to dry uniformly. Drywall surfaces that are not adequately sealed can cause paint to be absorbed more into poorly-sealed surface areas than well-sealed surface areas. The resulting uneven absorption of paint can cause color and sheen variations in the finish of the applied paint. For best results, use an oil-based primer/sealer to prime and seal new drywall.

Oil-based primer/sealers, at the time of the writing of this book, still offer a higher level of surface sealing than latex primer/sealers. They also offer the highest level of protection against the formation of paint bubbles (blisters) as applied paint dries over areas of sanded drywall joint compound. If oil-based products are no longer available in your area, use a high-quality latex primer/sealer that is capable of priming and sealing new drywall.

Avoid priming new drywall with a flat-finish latex paint. Flat-finish latex paint does not provide adequate surface sealing. Without consistent surface sealing, the color and sheen of applied paint may be prone to variation.

After the new drywall has been finished and sanded, remove sanding dust with a wiping cloth or towel, and then apply oil-based quick-drying primer/sealer. Allow drying, and then lightly sand dried primer/sealer using a pole sander with 100-grit or 120-grit pole sander paper. Smaller areas can be sanded with a sanding sponge. Remove sanding dust with a wiping cloth or towel, and then apply paint.

Sanding the dried primer/sealer helps to remove hardened, stubbly drywall cover fibers. It also helps to remove flecks. *(See Figure 5.23, on Page 89)*

Bare wood

New trim wood should be primed with an underbody primer, primer/sealer or White-Pigmented Shellac. Clear wood, free of knots and stains, should be primed with an underbody primer. If trim wood has stains, other than wood knots, prime it with an oil-based primer/sealer, or underbody primer that is also a sealer. White-Pigmented Shellac is effective for sealing wood knots. *(See section below- Bare wood with knots)* After primer/sealer or underbody has dried, lightly sand the wood with the fine grit-side of a sanding sponge, or 120-grit sandpaper. Remove sanding dust with a wiping cloth or towel, and then apply paint.

Note: If oil-based products are no longer available in your area, ask your paint dealer to recommend the best priming product for application over the type of wood that you need to prime.

Bare wood with knots

Seal wood knots with White-Pigmented Shellac. Several coats may be necessary to seal each wood knot. A disposable "one-use" paintbrush can be used to apply White-Pigmented Shellac. Follow manufacturer's directions for drying and re-coating.

Lightly sand the dried White-Pigmented Shellac with the fine grit-side of a sanding sponge, or 120-grit sandpaper. Remove sanding dust with a wiping cloth or towel before priming the entire piece of wood with an oil-based primer/sealer, or underbody primer. Allow drying. Lightly sand the dried primer/sealer. Remove sanding dust with a wiping cloth or towel, and then apply paint.

Painted wood with wood knot staining

Use White-Pigmented Shellac to seal wood knot staining on painted trim surfaces. Several coats may be necessary to seal each wood knot. Allow drying.

For best results, apply a coat of underbody primer or primer/sealer over the entire piece of trim or area of trim to establish a uniform substrate. Allow drying. Lightly sand the surface, and then remove sanding dust with a wiping cloth or towel before applying paint.

Section note: Slightly dampening the wiping cloth or towel will help to control dust when wiping sanded surfaces. After wiping, allow any surface moisture to dry before continuing surface preparation or applying paint, decorative paint, faux finish or stencils.

Spot priming and full coat priming

Definition

Spot priming is the application of primer or primer/sealer over a portion of the surface. A surface is often spot primed where it has a stain, or where it has been repaired. Wood surfaces with knots are often spot primed with White-Pigmented Shellac to cover just the areas with knots.

Full coat priming is the application of primer or primer/sealer over an entire surface, such as a ceiling, wall or piece of trim. Surfaces where a decorative painted finish, faux finish, painted mural or stencil will be applied should always be full coat primed.

Argument for full coat priming

Slight variations in the color and sheen of applied paint can occur overed spot primed areas. These variations are possible when paint is applied over differing substrates (one being the existing paint and the other being the spot primed area, or areas). The existing paint, and the primer or primer/sealer used to spot prime, may accept the color and sheen of the finish paint in differing ways. The application of dark-colored paints over differing substrates may result in more visible color and/or sheen variations than the application of light-colored paints applied over differing substrates. For best results, the entire ceiling, wall or trim surface should receive a full coat of primer or primer/sealer when several individual spots have been filled or repaired.

Possible exceptions

As there are often exceptions to every rule, the full coat application of primer, primer/sealer or White-Pigmented Shellac may not be necessary, or practical, in every situation. One possible exception to this rule is the application of White-Pigmented Shellac to seal wood knots before the application of trim paint. I have not seen a variation in the finish of trim surfaces when two coats of top-quality latex or oil-based trim paint are applied over a wood surface that has been spot primed with White-Pigmented Shellac. Your experience may be different. Another possible exception may occur on a surface that has had one, or only a few, small repairs. It may not be worth the time, effort and expense to prime an entire wall, ceiling or piece of trim for the sake of a few filled nail-sized holes, or small indentations.

Surface Prep Tip

Primer and sealer technology

Priming and sealing technology is rapidly changing. Oil-based primers and sealers are being replaced by VOC-compliant water-based "latex" versions. Oil-based primers and sealers are no longer available in some regions of the country. Ask your paint dealer to recommend their best primer, primer/sealer, underbody primer or sealer for each of your priming and sealing surface preparation tasks.

Rolling primers and primer/sealers

For best results, primers and primer/sealers should be rolled onto ceiling and wall surfaces. This is true because a rolled application of primer or primer/sealer will have a similar roller cover nap pattern to the existing surface, making the rolled primer or primer/sealer blend more effectively with the surrounding surface. A brushed application may show brush marks that are quite visible next to the existing roller cover nap pattern of the previous painting job.

Apply primer or primer/sealer to ceiling and wall surfaces with a 9" roller frame and ³/₈" nap roller cover. A slim roller frame and cover *(Fig. 5.42)* can be used for smaller applications. An extension rolling pole can be used with roller frames.

If you use a paintbrush to apply primer or primer/sealer to small areas on ceiling and wall surfaces, be sure to use light, long finishing strokes to reduce brush marks. Feather the edges of the application to eliminate any build ups or edge lines. Avoiding noticeable brush marks, build ups and edge lines will help the applied material to blend more successful with the surrounding surface.

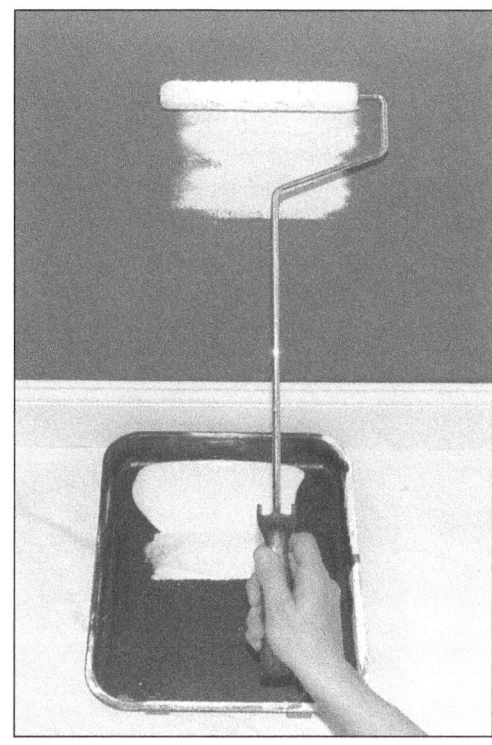

Figure 5.42
Slim roller frame and cover used to apply primer/sealer to a small surface area.

Surface Prep Tip

Do not skimp on priming and sealing

Do not cut corners when it comes to priming and sealing. Surfaces that are not properly primed and sealed often show clearly unacceptable results when painted.

TIPS AND TROUBLESHOOTING

Priming and Sealing

When possible, choose primers and primer/sealers that can be tinted to approximate the color of the paint you have chosen. Applying a tinted primer or primer/sealer helps paint color to be uniform over uneven surfaces.

Common Surface Preparation Repairs

This chapter covers the surface preparation repairs that are common to most interior house painting projects. These repairs fall into two categories: flush-fill repairs that require the flush-filling technique learned in *Chapter 5*, and another type of repair, called "non-flush" repairs.

A non-flush repair adds height to the surface. It involves the application of a repair material, such as a wall repair patch or self-adhesive mesh drywall joint tape, over a damaged area. Repair materials are covered with several coats of drywall joint compound to complete the repair. For good surface preparation results, non-flush repairs must be crafted so as to appear flush to the surface.

To help you successfully complete your surface preparation repairs, this chapter reveals the secrets of crafting virtually undetectable repairs. Mastery of surface preparation repairs will noticeably improve your surface preparation skill, and the look of your painted surfaces.

The common surface preparation repairs covered in this chapter are listed in *Table 6.1, on the next page.*

Topics covered in Chapter 6
Common Surface Preparation Repairs

		Page
1.	Concealing "non-flush" repairs by applying joint compound with correct shape and contour	110
2.	How to sand "non-flush" surface preparation repairs	113
3.	Repairing holes and damaged areas with a wall repair patch	115
4.	Repairing holes and indentations in wood surfaces with wood filler	120
5.	Repairing drywall nail pops	124
6.	Repair of surfaces with plastic anchors and metal Molly bolt jackets	131
7.	Supporting cracked ceiling drywall and refastening sagging ceiling drywall	134
8.	Repairing cracks with self-adhesive mesh drywall joint tape and drywall joint compound	142
9.	Tips for working with self-adhesive mesh drywall joint tape and drywall joint compound	149
10.	Repairing drywall cover damage	152

Table 6.1

CHAPTER 6 OBJECTIVES

1. Learning how to use a 6" taping knife to conceal "non-flush" repairs by applying joint compound with correct shape and contour.

2. Knowing how to sand "non-flush" surface preparation repairs.

3. Learning how to use an aluminum re-inforced wall repair patch to conceal holes and damaged areas.

4. Learn about wood filler and how to apply it to fill holes and indentations in wood trim surfaces.

5. The ability to repair nail pops.

6. Knowing how to repair surfaces that have plastic anchors and metal Molly bolt jackets. Also knowing when to call a handyman or other professional to remove fastening devices.

7. Understanding why cracked ceiling drywall should be supported by additional drywall nails or drywall screws before beginning ceiling crack repair.

8. Learning how to support the area around cracked ceiling drywall.

9. Learning how to support sagging ceiling drywall.

10. Learning crack repair.

11. Learning how to repair drywall cover damage that extends into the brown paper layer beneath the cover.

12. Mastering the common surface preparation repairs covered in this chapter.

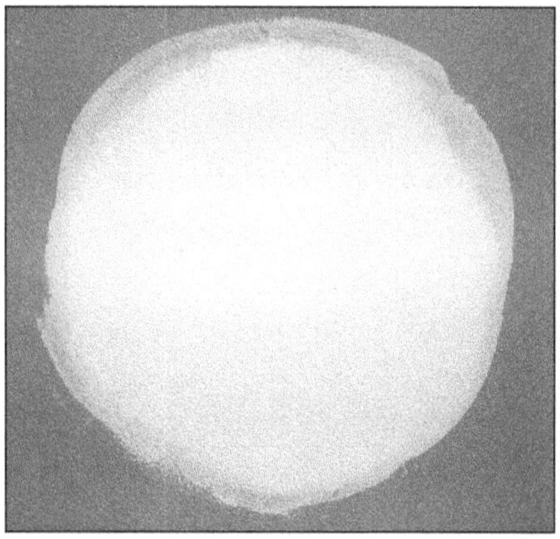

Figure 6.1
Round-shaped drywall joint compound application after four coats. (three full coats and one partial coat consisting of a few spot applications over a few small areas)

For more on partial coat joint compound applications, see Tip 9, on Page 66.

Thinness of the joint compound at the edges of the repair illustrates good contouring. Good joint compound contouring helps to conceal repairs and reduce sanding time and effort.

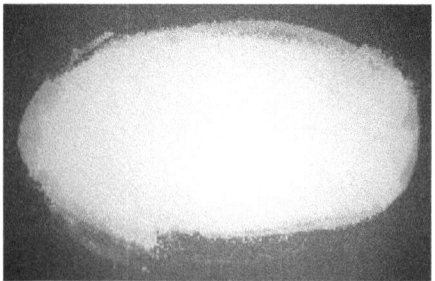

Figure 6.2
Oval-shaped drywall joint compound application after four coats.

CONCEALING NON-FLUSH REPAIRS BY APPLYING JOINT COMPOUND WITH CORRECT SHAPE AND CONTOUR

Shape

The first secret of crafting virtually undetectable non-flush surface preparation repairs is the application of drywall joint compound in a round or oval shape over repair materials, when possible. *(Figures 6.1 and 6.2)* The round or oval shape of applied joint compound avoids corners and straight lines that may be more easily detected with a square or rectangular-shaped application. A round-shaped application is ideal for concealing square-shaped repairs, such as a repair using an aluminum-reinforced wall repair patch. *(See Page 115)* An oval-shaped application is effective for concealing rectangular-shaped repairs, such as crack repair that extends from the corner of a door frame or header. *(See Figure 6.23, on Page 141 (shows crack) and Figure 6.37, on Page 147 (shows oval-shaped application))*

Notes: A round or oval-shaped joint compound application is not necessary for crack repairs over door headers or in corners. Applying joint compound in a rectangular shape with proper edge contouring will help you to conceal these repairs. *(See Figures 6.34 and 6.35, on Page 146)*

Skim coat applications that do not lend themselves to a round or oval shape should be crafted in shapes that have curved or rounded edges, when possible. Contouring the application helps to conceal the repair. *(See Contour below & Figure 5.15, on Page 78)*

Contour

The second secret of crafting virtually undetectable non-flush surface preparation repairs is the correct contouring of joint compound over repair materials. Joint compound should be applied flat over repair materials, or the surface when skim coating, with a gradual sloping at the edge of the repair towards the surrounding surface. The repair should be thinnest at the edges. *(Figures 6.1 and 6.2)* Contouring joint compound helps to conceal the repair area, as the eye is less likely to notice the gradual sloping of a properly contoured repair. A contour area equal to approximately one-half to one-full taping knife blade width will conceal most repairs. Small repairs, such as corner crack repairs, can be contoured just at the edges. Skillful sanding will maintain the correct repair-concealing contour. *(See HOW TO SAND NON-FLUSH SURFACE PREPARATION REPAIRS, on Page 113)*

Note: Additional coats of joint compound extending several inches beyond repair materials may be needed to make the repair blend into an uneven or slightly curved repair surface. In these situations, the contour should start after the repair appears to have taken the shape of the surrounding surface.

What's Needed to Apply Joint Compound in a Round or Oval Shape with Correct Contour

Applying joint compound in a round or oval shape with correct contour requires the following:

6" Taping knife with a flexible blade

A 6" taping knife with a flexible blade enables the control and dexterity needed for the easy application of joint compound in a round or oval shape over repair materials. It also provides the ability to contour applied joint compound on virtually any shaped application with little, if any, excess application.
Note: A 4" or 6" flexible blade taping knife is also the best tool for a rectangular-shaped application with correct contour. *(See Figures 6.34 and 6.35, on Page 146)*

The ability to flex the taping knife blade to contour the joint compound application

The ability to gently flex the blade of the taping knife while applying joint compound is the secret of good non-flush repair joint compound application technique. A gently-flexed taping knife blade enables precise joint compound application in round and oval shapes with correctly contouring. This technique requires practice, but can be learned quickly. Students in my surface preparation classes have shown proficiency in flexing the blade and applying joint compound in round and oval shapes, with proper contouring, during the second day of class.

How to Flex the Taping Knife Blade to Make Round and Oval-Shaped Contoured Applications with Virtually No Excess Application

1. While making an arc, gently apply pressure to the outside edge of the taping knife blade. This is done by turning your hand slightly in the direction of the outside edge. The resulting hand motion will gently, and only slightly, flex the taping knife blade. The inside edge of the blade will lift approximately 1/8" from the surface as the outside edge is pressed against the surface. *(Figure 6.3)* The gentle pressure exerted on the outside edge produces a contoured shape to the applied joint compound. It also gives you a coat of joint compound with virtually no excess application. Properly contoured joint compound will begin to dry on the edge in only a few minutes.

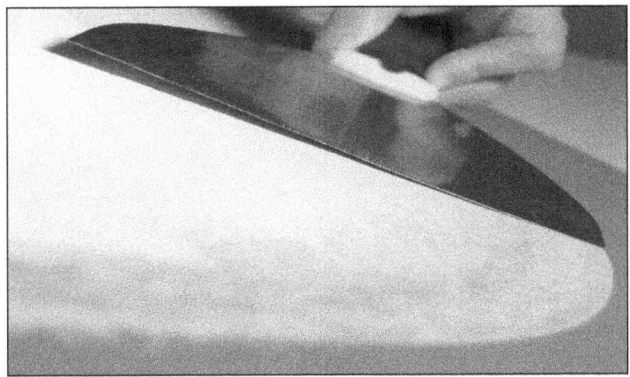

Figure 6.3
Contouring applied joint compound with good taping knife technique. Hand is applying slight pressure towards the edge of the applied joint compound. Notice the thinness of the joint compound at the edge of the repair.

Tool angle

In *Chapter 5*, using the taping knife at approximately a 45-degree angle to the surface is recommended for the flush-filling technique shown in *Diagram 5.1, on Page 61*. *(See Tip 3, on Page 62)*

For the shaping and contouring of applied drywall joint compound, you may find it easier to make an arc while holding the taping knife closer to the surface. *(See Figure 6.3, on previous page)* Experiment to find the best tool angle that enables you to make oval and circular arcs.

2. Continue to make arcs until your round or oval shape is complete.
   (See Figures 6.1 and 6.2, on Page 110)

Tips and Troubleshooting

Using shape and contour to conceal non-flush surface preparation repairs

1. Learning to apply drywall joint compound while gently flexing the taping knife blade takes time and practice. Achieving a gradual contouring of applied joint compound to conceal repairs is a technique that will greatly improve your interior surface preparation. Skillful application of joint compound will also reduce sanding time and effort.

2. Practice making shaped and contoured round, oval, and rectangular-shaped drywall joint compound applications.

How to sand non-flush surface preparation repairs

The third secret of crafting virtually undetectable non-flush surface preparation repairs is skillful sanding. The tool that enables precise sanding of non-flush surface preparation repairs is the sanding sponge. The sanding sponge is also the best tool for sanding flush-fills, which were covered in *Chapter 5*.

Why a sanding sponge should be used to sand non-flush repairs

The features of the sanding sponge make it the best sanding tool for non-flush repairs. Its block-like shape and flexible inner foam core are ideal for sanding shaped and contoured repairs, and its small size makes it easy to manipulate and maneuver. A fine/medium combination grit sanding sponge has one edge and one side with fine abrasive grit, and one edge and one side with medium grit. This two-grit combination enables you to simply turn the sanding sponge to an edge or side to utilize the sanding surface that you need. Sanding sponges come in varying sizes, and some are available with beveled edges. *(For more information on sanding sponges, turn back to Page 91)*

Why a sanding sponge is the better choice over other sanding tools when sanding non-flush repairs

Pole sander- The large, rigid sanding platform on a pole sander can not match the sanding sponge's ability to enable quick and precise sanding of shaped and contoured repairs. And to change grit levels, one must remove the sandpaper screw clamps and place a different piece of sandpaper onto the platform, and then re-fasten the screw clamps. The size of the platform is also a disadvantage as it may tend to remove too much dried joint compound from the repair with each sanding pass. The large size of the platform may also prevent the pole sander from being able to completely sand edges or imperfections on slightly varied, or contoured surfaces. *(For more information on the pole sander, turn back to Page 91)*

Sanding platform or sanding block- As with the pole sander, the size and rigidity of the sanding platform and sanding block may be a disadvantage when working on slightly varied, or contoured surfaces. Even a small sanding block wrapped with sandpaper is no match for a sanding sponge. And to change grit levels when using either a sanding platform or sanding block, one must replace the sandpaper. Another potential problem encountered when using sanding platforms and sanding blocks is the curling of sandpaper at the edges of the platform or block. Sandpaper that has edge-curled will often leave "scratch" marks or linear indentations where it has made contact with the repair surface.

Sandpaper- Repairs sanded with hand-held sandpaper often show ridges or uneven areas where fingers exerted pressure during sanding. If you do use sandpaper to sand repairs, you will get somewhat better results if you fold the sandpaper as shown in *Figures 5.24 - 5.26, on Page 90*. For best results, choose a sanding sponge over sandpaper when sanding non-flush surface preparation repairs.

Technique for sanding non-flush repairs

Well-crafted repairs have a flat top, contoured slope and edge. Sand each part carefully to maintain the repair's shape, contour and coverage of repair materials. Well-crafted repairs often require only minimal sanding.

Step One

Use the fine-grit side of your sanding sponge to sand the edge (outer half-inch, or less) of the repair. Follow the shape of the repair when sanding. The edge can be divided into two or more sections for easier sanding. The edge of the repair will often require the most sanding effort. If a build-up of joint compound exists, start sanding with the medium-grit side of your sanding sponge. A slight increase in hand pressure on the sanding sponge will help you to more quickly sand any edge build-ups.

Step Two

Use the fine-grit side to gently sand the contoured area of the repair. As in *Step One*, follow the shape of the repair when sanding. Back-and-forth sanding strokes with light pressure on the sanding sponge work best. The contoured area can be divided into two or more sections for easier sanding. When possible, keep the entire sanding sponge in contact with the surface while sanding.

Step Three

Use the fine-grit side to sand the flat top of the repair using straight, back-and-forth sanding stokes with light pressure on the sanding sponge. Stop after every few stokes to check your progress.

Step Four

Remove sanding dust from the repair with a wiping cloth or towel. Removal of sanding dust may reveal areas of the repair that need additional joint compound, or additional sanding. If the shape or contour of the repair has been compromised by sanding, or if repair materials have become visible, apply joint compound.

Removing sanding dust also helps to prevent flecks. *(For more information on flecks, turn back to Page 89)*

TIPS AND TROUBLESHOOTING

Sanding non-flush repairs

1. After the edges of the repair have been sanded, use only light strokes with minimal pressure on the sanding sponge when sanding the flat top and contoured area of the repair. Avoid sanding too fast or too vigorously so as to not expose repair materials or compromise the shape and contour of the repair.

2. Stop after every few strokes to check your work.

3. After sanding, remove sanding dust with a wiping cloth or towel.

4. Apply additional joint compound if repair material has been exposed, the shape and/or contour of the repair has been compromised, or if indentations and imperfections are present. A partial, or spot, application of joint compound may be necessary.
(See Tip 9, on Page 66)

Repairing holes and damaged areas with a wall repair patch

A wall repair patch is made of a thin square of aluminum that is covered by a slightly larger square of self-adhesive mesh tape. *(Figure 6.4)* The back of the repair patch also has an adhesive coating for fastening the patch to the repair surface. Wall repair patches are available in four-inch, six-inch and eight-inch sizes.

The wall repair patch can be used to cover holes, indentations and damaged areas in both drywall and plaster surfaces. Surface damage that can be covered with a wall repair patch may include drywall cover damage. *(See Page 157, Tip Number 1)*

DO NOT cover wet, moist, mildewed or mold-affected surfaces with a wall repair patch.

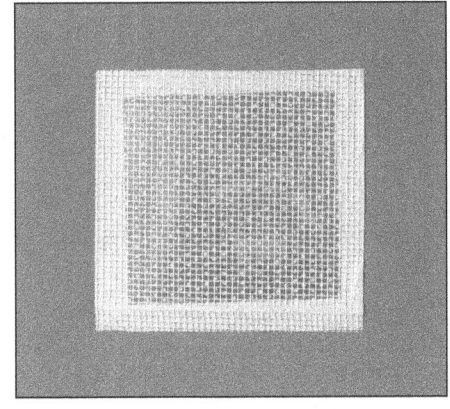

Figure 6.4
Aluminum-reinforced wall repair patch.

Limits of wall patch repairs

Wall patch repairs should not be subjected to the weight-bearing demands of nails, screws or picture-hanging hardware. These repairs may fail under the weight of any load. Attempting to drive a nail or fasten a screw into a wall repair patch can damage the aluminum square causing failure of the repair. **DO NOT** use a wall repair patch on any ceiling or wall surface where you may later install plant hooks, pictures, wall hangings, curtain rods, valances, light fixtures, stereo speakers or other accessories.

Using a wall repair patch on a surface before the application of decorative paint, faux finish, mural art or stencils

Due to the limits of wall patch repairs, care should be taken in the decision to use a wall repair patch to repair a ceiling or wall surface where decorative paint, faux finish, mural art or stencils will be applied. If a nail or screw is driven into a surface repaired by a wall patch, significant, and possibly irreparable, damage can occur to decorative paint, faux finish, mural artwork and stencil art. For best results, avoid the use of a wall repair patch on surfaces where decorative paint, faux finish, mural art or stencils will be applied. Instead, repair drywall surfaces using drywall, and plaster surfaces with plastering materials applied by a licensed professional plastering contractor.

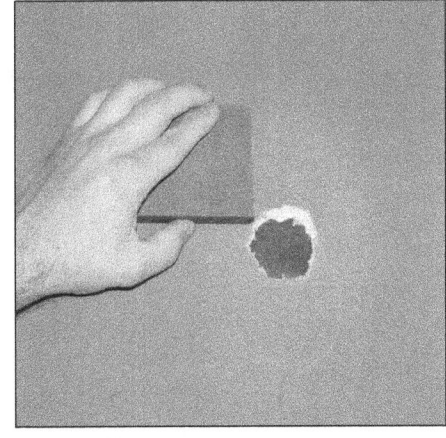

Figure 6.5
A sanding sponge is used to smooth the border of the hole. It is then used to sand the repair surface around the hole.

Sanding the border of the hole until it is smooth will help the wall patch to lie flat on the surface.

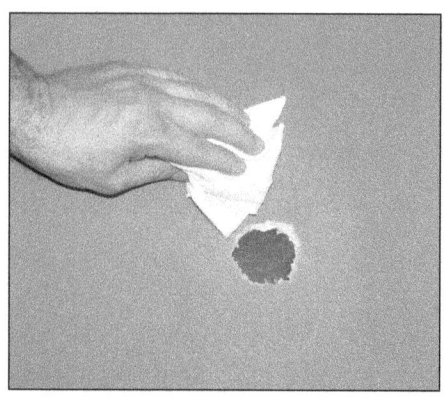

Figure 6.6
Remove dust from the repair surface with a wiping cloth.

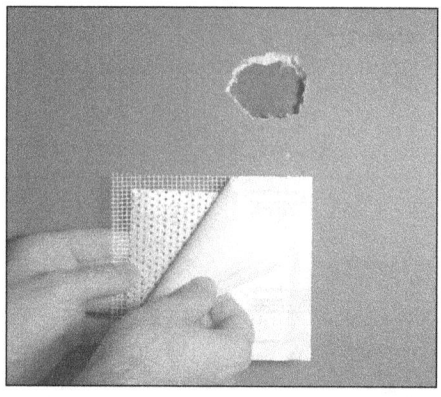

Figure 6.7
Removing the liner from the wall repair patch.

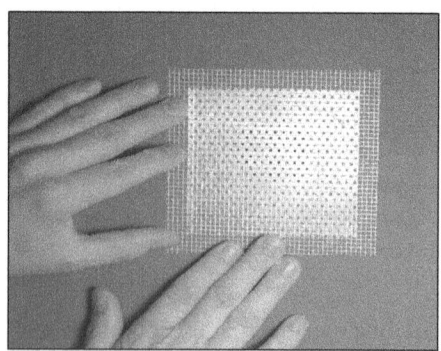

Figure 6.8
Center the wall patch over the repair area.

Tools and materials

Eye and respiratory system protection, aluminum-reinforced wall repair patch, 6" taping knife, putty knife, scraper, mud tray and joint compound, fine/medium-grit sanding sponge, roller frame and extension rolling pole with ³/₈" nap roller cover or slim roller frame and roller cover, rolling pan, wiping cloth or towel, oil-based quick-drying primer/sealer, empty paint can, "all paints" paintbrush, paint thinner and hand cleaner.

Steps

1. Wear eye and respiratory system protection.
   (*See Pages 19-20 for eye and respiratory system protection information*)

2. Remove any loose debris from the repair area using a putty knife or scraper.

3. Use the medium-grit side of a fine/medium sanding sponge to sand the border (edge) of the damage. Also sand the area where the repair will be located. (wall patch and joint compound) *(Figure 6.5, on previous page)*

4. Remove sanding dust with a wiping cloth or towel. *(Figure 6.6)* Slightly dampening the wiping cloth or towel will help to control dust. Allow any surface moisture to dry before going to *Step 5*.

5. Remove the liner from the wall patch. *(Figure 6.7)*

6. Center the aluminum square of the wall patch over the repair area. Holes and damaged areas should be covered by the aluminum square. Press gently on the wall patch to fasten it to the surface. *(Figure 6.8)* Avoid applying pressure where the wall patch cannot adhere to the repair surface, such as over a hole. Applying pressure over a hole or damaged area may cause the aluminum square to bend. Discard bent wall patches.

7. Use a putty knife to load a small amount of joint compound into a mud tray. Apply the first coat of joint compound over the wall patch using a 6" taping knife. Joint compound application should be circular in shape around the wall patch, filling the mesh but not covering the tape completely. Extend the joint compound application approximately two inches beyond the wall patch.

8. Allow drying. Joint compound is dry when white.

9. Apply a second coat of joint compound in a round shape over the repair area, extending an inch or two beyond the first application. Use the taping knife to contour the joint compound so that it begins to conceal the height of the repair. Properly contoured joint compound will be thinnest at the edges. The mesh tape should be slightly visible after the second coat of joint compound. *(See Pages 110-111 for information about shaping and contouring joint compound over repairs)*

10. Allow drying.

11. Apply a third coat of joint compound extending an inch or two beyond the edges of the last application. Continue to contour the joint compound to help conceal the height of the repair. The wall patch should now be completely covered with joint compound. Allow drying. *(Figure 6.9)* Apply an additional coat of joint compound should any part of the wall patch be visible. Six and eight-inch wall patch repairs often require four or more applications of joint compound. Uneven repair surfaces will also often require more than three coats of joint compound.

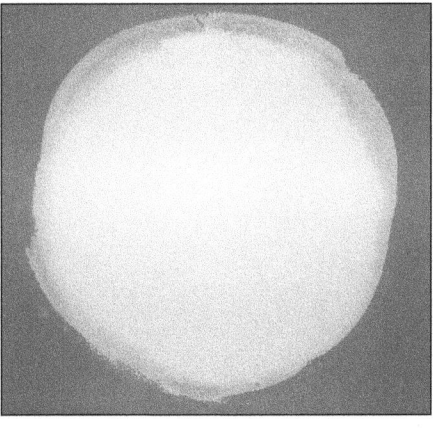

Figure 6.9
Wall patch repair ready for sanding. This repair required four applications of joint compound, the last being only a partial coat. Notice the thinness of the joint compound at the edges.

12. Lightly sand the dried repair with the fine-grit side of a fine/medium sanding sponge. (*See* How to sand non-flush surface preparation repairs, on Pages 113-114)

13. Remove sanding dust with a wiping cloth or towel. Slightly dampening the wiping cloth or towel will help to control dust. Allow any surface moisture to dry before going to *Step 14*.

14. Stir then pour oil-based quick-drying primer/sealer into an empty paint can. Two or three inches in the paint can will usually be enough to complete any cutting in if the wall patch repair is close to a corner or wood trim. Apply a coat of oil-based quick-drying primer/sealer over the wall patch repair using a slim roller frame and cover or 9" roller frame, ³/₈" nap roller cover and extension rolling pole. Allow drying.

Note: If oil-based products are no longer available in your area, use a high-quality latex primer/sealer in this step. Follow directions for cleaning tools, hands and skin. Wear any recommended respiratory system protection.

Note: If other preparation or repair work will be done, then apply primer/sealer in this room or part of the project after all preparation and repair work has been completed.

15. Lightly sand the dried primer/sealer with the fine-grit side of a sanding sponge.

16. Remove sanding dust with a wiping cloth or towel. Slightly dampening the wiping cloth or towel will help to control dust. Allow any surface moisture to dry before going to *Step 17*.

17. Apply paint, decorative paint, faux finish or stencil.

Refer to Chapter 1 for information regarding safety and avoiding spontaneous combustion fire when using paint thinner, turpentine, mineral spirits, denatured alcohol, paint deglosser, oil-based primers and primer/sealers and White-Pigmented Shellac.

Chapter 6 Common Surface Preparation Repairs

Estimated Time to Complete this Technique

The estimated time to complete a wall patch repair is two days. The actual working time will be approximately one hour. Applying joint compound coats continuously after drying will enable some repairs to be completed within one day.

Note: Estimated time to complete method steps includes drying times for repair compounds and primer/sealer. Refer to the directions on the container for drying times of repair compounds and primer/sealer. Humid conditions will lengthen drying times. Other preparation and repair work can be done in the room while waiting for repair compounds to dry.

TIPS AND TROUBLESHOOTING

Repairing holes and damaged areas with a wall repair patch

1. For best results, avoid using more than one wall repair patch to cover a hole or damaged area. Damaged areas larger than one wall patch should be repaired with either a larger wall patch, drywall replacement or plaster repair.

2. The wall repair patch should be fastened to a solid surface on each of its four sides.

3. Avoid using a wall repair patch to cover holes or damaged areas on wood surfaces.

4. **DO NOT** use a wall repair patch to cover wet, moist, mildewed or mold-affected surfaces.

5. To conceal wall patch repairs over uneven surfaces, additional coats of drywall joint compound that extend the total application 6-8 inches, or more, beyond the edges of the wall patch may be required.

6. A wall repair patch can often be used to repair the hole left after the removal of a room intercom speaker.

REPAIRING HOLES AND INDENTATIONS IN WOOD SURFACES WITH WOOD FILLER

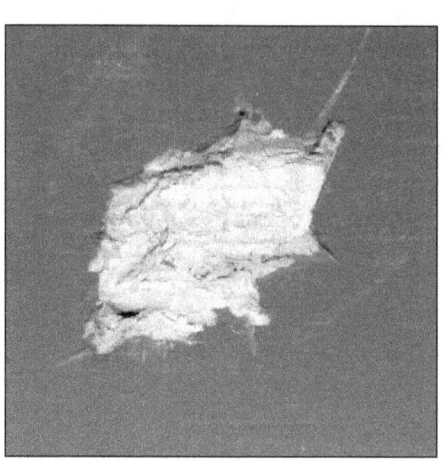

Figure 6.10
Damage to wood surface measures approximately 1½" long and ⅜" deep.

Wood filler can be used to repair holes and indentations in wood surfaces. *(Figure 6.10)* Its hard, durable finish makes it ideal for deep and wide wood surface repairs. Use a two-part wood filler for weight-bearing repairs.

Note: Some holes and indentations may not be repairable with wood filler. If damage is too deep or wide, wood replacement may be necessary. Consult with a licensed carpenter whenever you have concern about the soundness or repairability of a wood surface.

Tools and materials

Eye and respiratory system protection, wood filler, 4" or 6" taping knife, putty knife, scraper, fine/medium-grit sanding sponge, wiping cloth or towel, oil-based quick-drying primer/sealer, empty paint can, "all paints" paintbrush, paint thinner and hand cleaner.

Steps

1. Wear eye and respiratory system protection.
   (See Pages 19-20 for eye and respiratory system protection information)

2. Remove any loose paint and surface material with a putty knife or scraper.

3. Sand the repair area using the medium-grit side of a sanding sponge or 80-grit sandpaper. Be sure that the border (edge) of the damaged area is flush with the surrounding surface.

4. Remove sanding dust with a wiping cloth or towel. Slightly dampening the wiping cloth or towel will help to control dust. Allow any surface moisture to dry before going to *Step 5*.

5. **For small fills-** Apply wood filler flush to the surface using a putty knife or taping knife. *(Figure 6.11)* Remove excess. Allow drying.

   For deep and wide fills- Follow the directions on the container concerning the layering of deep and wide fills. Apply first layer. Remove excess. Allow drying.

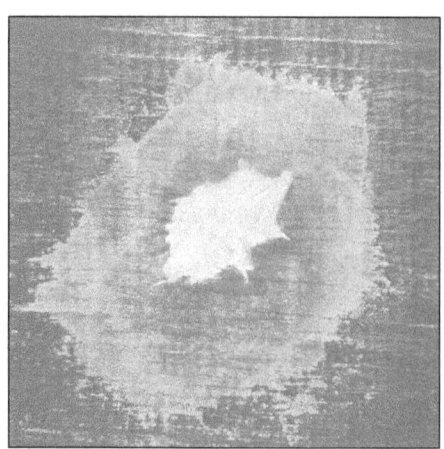

Figure 6.11
Damaged area after the application of wood filler.

6. **For small fills-** If shrinkage has occurred, apply a coat of wood filler or a coat of spackling compound flush to the surface. Remove excess. Allow drying.

   For deep and wide fills- Follow the directions on the container concerning the layering of deep and wide fills. Apply second layer. Remove excess. Allow drying.

7. **For small fills-** You should be ready for *Step 8*. If not, repeat *Step 6*.

   For deep and wide fills- Follow the directions on the container concerning the layering of deep and wide fills. Apply a coat of spackling compound flush to the surface. Remove excess. Allow drying.

8. Sand dried wood filler with the medium-grit side of a sanding sponge. Then finish sand with the fine-grit side. In some instances, you may have to begin sanding with folded 50- or 60-grit sandpaper. *(See Folding sandpaper, on Page 90)*

   Sand spackling compound with the fine-grit side of a sanding sponge.

9. Remove sanding dust with a wiping cloth or towel. Slightly dampening the wiping cloth or towel will help to control dust. Allow any surface moisture to dry before going to *Step 10*.

10. Stir then pour oil-based quick-drying primer/sealer into an empty paint can. An inch or two in the paint can will usually be enough to prime the filled holes and indentations in several rooms. Apply a coat of oil-based quick-drying primer/sealer over completed repairs. A slim roller frame, roller cover and rolling pan can be used to apply primer/sealer over large areas such as shelves, flat doors and bay windowsills. Allow drying.

    Note: If oil-based products are no longer available in your area, use a high-quality latex primer/sealer capable of priming and sealing wood filler in this step. Follow directions for cleaning tools, hands and skin. Wear any recommended respiratory system protection.

    Note: If other preparation or repair work will be done in this room or area, then apply primer/sealer in this room or part of the project after all preparation and repair work has been completed.

11. Lightly sand dried primer/sealer with the fine-grit side of a sanding sponge. Then remove sanding dust with a wiping cloth or towel. Slightly dampening the wiping cloth or towel will help to control dust. Allow any surface moisture to dry before going to *Step 12*.

12. Apply paint, decorative paint, faux finish or stencil.

More wood filling

Wood filler can be used for larger surface fills on wood trim. *(Figure 6.12)*

Figure 6.12
Using wood filler to repair a door frame after hinge removal.

Refer to Chapter 1 for information regarding safety and avoiding spontaneous combustion fire when using paint thinner, turpentine, mineral spirits, denatured alcohol, paint deglosser, oil-based primers and primer/sealers and White-Pigmented Shellac.

Estimated Time to Complete this Technique

The estimated time to complete a wood filler repair is usually less than one day. The actual working time will be approximately 10-15 minutes for each fill. Deep fills requiring two coats of wood filler will require additional working and drying time.

Note: Estimated time to complete method steps includes drying times for repair compounds and primer/sealer. Refer to the directions on the container for drying times of repair compounds and primer/sealer. Humid conditions will lengthen drying times. Other preparation and repair work can be done in the room while waiting for repair compounds to dry.

Tips and Troubleshooting

Wood filling

1. Work with small amounts of wood filler. Wood filler is more easily spread and controlled when working with small amounts.

2. Apply only enough wood filler to flush-fill holes and indentations. Wood filler requires more effort to sand than other repair compounds. Remove all excess application.

3. After the first coat of wood filler has dried, spackling compound may be used to fill areas of shrinkage. (flush to the surface) For slight shrinkage, a coat of spackling compound will be easier to apply than a coat of wood filler. For deep and wide repairs, a second coat, or layer, of wood filler should be applied. *(See Tip 6)*

4. Two-part wood fillers have a working time, or "pot life," of only a few minutes. When using a two-part wood filler, mix only the amount of wood filler that can be used within the working time listed on the container.

5. When using a two-part wood filler, stop application once the wood filler begins to stiffen. Discard stiffening wood filler and clean tools before mixing another batch.

6. For deep and wide surface repairs, follow directions on the wood filler container pertaining to layering and drying times for deep and wide repairs. Deep and wide holes and indentations should be filled with two coats of wood filler. When layering these repairs, allow sufficient time for the first coat (layer) to dry before applying a second coat. Insufficient drying of wood filler layers often delays the curing process, causing the repair to continue to shrink over time as curing occurs. Apply the second coat of wood filler flush to the surface. After the second coat has dried, spackling compound may be used to fill slight areas of shrinkage flush to the surface.

7. Clean application tools after use. Dried wood filler is difficult to remove from tools.

Repairing drywall nail pops

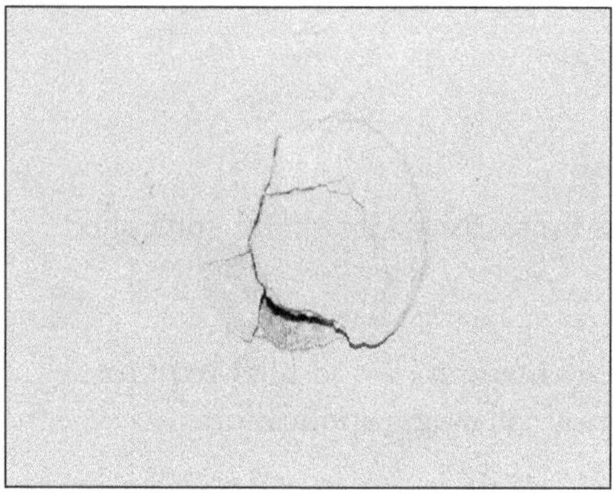

Before the widespread use of drywall screws, drywall was fastened with drywall nails. Early drywall nails had a smooth shaft (without grip-enhancing rings) and lacked the holding power of today's drywall screws and ringed drywall nails. During drywall installation, drywall nails were hammered into place and driven approximately 1/8" below the surface creating a drywall nail "dimple." The dimple was filled with two or three coats of drywall joint compound during the finishing process. The dried joint compound, when sanded, made the dimple flush to the surface and ready for priming and painting.

Figure 6.13
Surface damage caused by a nail pop.

Nail pop definition

A nail pop is the loosening of a drywall nail from its dimple. Over time, drywall nail loosening will often cause the drywall joint compound and paint directly over a nail pop to bulge and crack, as seen in *Figure 6.13*. Early drywall nails are prone to popping from their dimples during structural movement and settling. An unusually cold winter or rainy spring will often cause a few drywall nails to pop.

Before beginning nail pop repair: Warning for hammer use

Repairing nail pops often requires the use of a hammer. Hammering causes surface vibrations that can dislodge pictures, artworks, wall hangings, ceiling hangings, floor items, shelf items and table items in the room where you are working, and adjacent rooms. Dislodged items may tip or fall causing damage to the item, other possessions, interior surfaces, furniture and flooring surfaces.

Remove or secure all pictures, artworks, wall hangings, ceiling hangings, shelf items, table items, and all other items that may fall, tip or break, in the room where you are working, and adjacent rooms, before beginning nail pop repair. Use caution and restraint when hammering nail pops near, electronic equipment, computers, electrical fixtures, electrical switches and outlets, and thermostats.

Wall-mounted electronic devices, such as televisions and stereo equipment, may also be damaged due to surface vibrations from hammering.

Refastening sagging ceiling drywall

Numerous nail pops on a ceiling may indicate the need to refasten sagging ceiling drywall.
(See SUPPORTING CRACKED CEILING DRYWALL AND REFASTENING SAGGING CEILING DRYWALL, ON PAGE *134*)

Tools and materials

Eye and respiratory system protection, drywall hammer or hammer, Cat's Paw tool, drill driver with magnetic drive guide, 1³/₈" drywall screws or drywall nails, 6" taping knife, putty knife, scraper, mud tray and drywall joint compound, fine/medium-grit sanding sponge, wiping cloth, oil-based quick-drying primer/sealer, empty paint can, "all paints" paintbrush, slim roller frame and cover or 9" roller frame with ³/₈" nap roller cover and extension rolling pole, rolling pan, paint thinner and hand cleaner.

Steps

1. Wear eye and respiratory system protection.
   (See Pages 19-20 for eye and respiratory system protection information)

2. Remove the popped nail with the claw on the back of the hammer, or a Cat's Paw tool if the nail has lifted far enough from the surface to dislodge the drywall joint compound covering it, as shown in *Figure 6.13, on opposite page*. Rusted nails should also be removed. Place a paint stirring stick under the claw of your hammer or the claw or your Cat's Paw tool to protect the surface during nail removal. *(See Figure 6.16, on Page 129)* A rusted drywall nail can indicate an ongoing water leak. *(See Chapter 3: Tasks to Complete Before Surface Preparation Begins)*

3. If the nail was removed, use a drill driver with magnetic drive guide to drive a 1³/₈" drywall screw into the nail hole. To provide extra support for the nail pop repair, drive a screw two inches on ether side of the repair along the ceiling joist or wall stud as shown in *Figure. 6.14*. Drywall screws should be driven just below the surface. Remove the 1³/₈" drywall screw and use a 1¼" drywall screw if the 1³/₈" drywall screw can not be driven just below the surface.

4. If the drywall nail did not need removal *(in Step 2)*, use a drywall hammer, or hammer, to re-dimple the drywall nail approximately ¹/₈" below the surface. *(Fig. 6.15, on next page)* Avoid dimpling the drywall nail more than ¹/₈," as deeper dimples may damage (tear) the drywall cover and require more effort to fill. Two or three light to moderate hammer strokes should be sufficient to dimple a drywall nail to a depth of approximately ¹/₈." For extra support along the repair, drive a drywall screw two inches on ether side of the repair. *(See Fig. 6.14)* Drywall screws should be driven just below the surface.

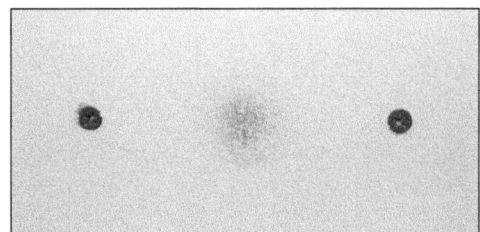

Fig. 6.14
Drywall screws give extra support to a nail pop repair, helping to keep the repair intact.

5. Use a putty knife to remove any cracked or loosened surface material after hammering or driving screws. Remove fine debris with a duster. Apply joint compound with a 6" taping knife to fill nail dimples or cover driven screws. Use the flush-filling technique shown in *Diagram 5.1, on Page 61*.

6. When uniformly white, joint compound is dry and ready for a second coat. Apply and allow drying. If necessary, apply a third coat of joint compound to fill the dimple or area above the driven screws flush to the surface.

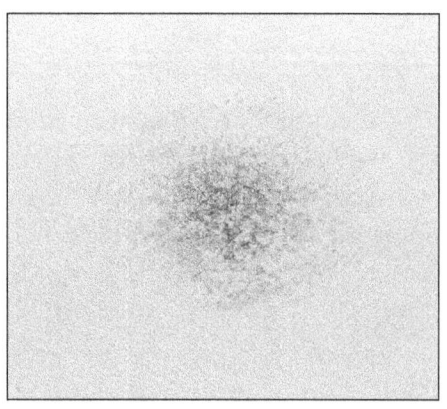

Figure 6.15
Use a drywall hammer to re-dimple a nail pop.

Note: A hammer can also be used to re-dimple a drywall nail pop. The drywall hammer is a better tool for this repair because its rounded head is designed to make dimples.

7. Lightly sand the dried joint compound with the fine-grit side of a sanding sponge.

8. Remove sanding dust with a wiping cloth or towel. Slightly dampening the wiping cloth or towel will help to control dust. Allow any surface moisture to dry before going to *Step 9*.

   Apply an additional coat of drywall joint compound if the sanded repair is not flush to the surface, allow drying, sand, and then repeat *Step 8*.

9. Stir then pour oil-based quick-drying primer/sealer into an empty paint can. Two or three inches in the paint can will usually be enough to complete the cutting in of one ceiling or wall surface where nail pop repairs are located. Apply a coat of oil-based quick-drying primer/sealer over the repaired surface using a 9" roller frame, ³/₈" nap roller cover and extension rolling pole. A slim roller frame and roller cover can be used for smaller areas. *(See Slim roller frame and cover in Figure 5.42, on Page 105)* Allow drying.

   Note: If oil-based products are no longer available in your area, use a high-quality latex primer/sealer in this step. Follow directions for cleaning tools, hands and skin. Wear any recommended respiratory system protection.

   Note: If other preparation or repair work will be done, then apply primer/sealer in this room or part of the project after all preparation and repair work has been completed.

10. Lightly sand the dried primer/sealer with the fine-grit side of a sanding sponge. Entire ceiling and wall surfaces can be sanded using a pole sander with 100-grit or 120-grit pole sander paper.

11. Remove sanding dust with a wiping cloth or towel. Slightly dampening the wiping cloth or towel will help to control dust. Allow any surface moisture to dry before going to *Step 12*.

12. Apply paint, decorative paint, faux finish or stencil.

Refer to Chapter 1 for information regarding safety and avoiding spontaneous combustion fire when using paint thinner, turpentine, mineral spirits, denatured alcohol, paint deglosser, oil-based primers and primer/sealers and White-Pigmented Shellac.

Estimated Time to Complete this Technique

The estimated time to complete a nail pop repair is less than one day. The actual working time will be approximately fifteen minutes.

Note: Estimated time to complete steps includes drying times for repair compounds and primer/sealer. Refer to the directions on the container for drying times of repair compounds and primer/sealer. Humid conditions will lengthen drying times. Other preparation and repair work can be done in the room while waiting for repair compounds to dry.

Surface Prep Tip

Avoid applying excessive amounts of drywall joint compound when crafting surface preparation repairs

One of the biggest obstacles to crafting good surface preparation repairs is the excessive application of drywall joint compound.

Excessive joint compound application on surface preparation repairs was one of my biggest challenges as a beginning painting contractor. I often applied joint compound in thick layers over repair materials. My thick applications, at times, developed air bubble holes and cracks during drying. And needless to say, I did quite a bit of sanding.

A more experienced painting contractor taught me how to apply thinner layers of joint compound. He preferred "building up" the repair slowly, instead of my ill-advised method of excessive application followed by long sessions of arduous sanding. He was right. This lesson caused me to change my application technique. From then on, I applied thinner coats of joint compound to build up repairs. Then my surface preparation repairs actually looked better, and required much less sanding effort.

Try applying joint compound in thinner layers if you are having difficulty sanding your surface preparation repairs. If your dried applications have air bubble holes and cracks, you **need** to apply thinner coats. Even if it takes an extra coat or two- you will be glad when you see how much better your repairs look, and how much less sanding you need to do.

For a review of drywall joint compound application instruction, see the following sections:

Using a 6" taping knife to apply repair compounds, on Pages 60-61

Tips for skillful taping knife use, on Pages 62-63

Application of drywall joint compound, on Pages 64-66

Surface Prep Tip: *Applying repair compounds*, on Page 67

Skim coating, on Page 76

Skim coating ceiling and wall surfaces with drywall joint compound, on Pages 77-81

Concealing non-flush repairs by applying joint compound with correct shape and contour, on Pages 110-112

TIPS AND TROUBLESHOOTING

Nail pop repair

1. Place a wooden paint stirring stick under your hammer or Cat's Paw tool to protect surfaces from damage when removing nails and screws. *(Figure 6.16)*

2. Avoid excessive hammering, or "over-dimpling," of drywall nails. Excessive hammering causes deep dimples that require additional coats of joint compound to flush-fill. It may also cause drywall cover damage.

3. Try using a drywall hammer for re-dimpling nail pops. The rounded head of the drywall hammer is designed to make the correct dimple. Its rounded head design also helps to prevent the tearing of the drywall cover that can result from over-hammering a drywall nail dimple with a claw hammer.

4. If you have many nail pop dimples to fill, try a lightweight joint compound. Lightweight joint compound shrinks less as it dries than regular weight joint compound. You may be able to fill the dimples with less coats of lightweight joint compound.

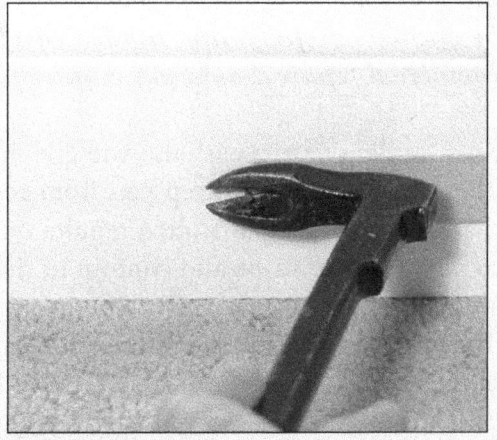

Figure 6.16
Stirring stick protects wood surface during nail removal with a Cat's Paw tool. This technique can also be used when pulling out a drywall nail.

Surface Prep Tip

Careful sanding of completed repairs

Another topic that merits review is the careful sanding of completed repairs. Repairs should be crafted carefully, and sanded carefully. When joint compound is properly applied, a completed repair should not require prolonged and arduous sanding.

Start sanding repairs with the fine-grit side of a fine/medium-grit combination sanding sponge. The fine-grit side will keep you from removing too much dried joint compound. Remember that well-crafted repairs often require only minimal sanding- so sand carefully. Also remember to maintain the shape and contour of the repair, and coverage of repair materials.

The medium-grit side is best used, if needed, to sand the edge, or border, of the repair. The edge of the repair is often the area that needs the most sanding. If you use the medium-grit side, take care not to sand too vigorously. Then finish sand with the fine-grit side.

Sand repairs using light to moderate applied pressure on the sanding sponge, stopping after every few sanding strokes to check your work. Wipe the surface of the repair with a wiping cloth or towel. After sanding dust removal, check your progress. You may find that portions of the repair have been adequately sanded and that other areas need more attention. Sand until the repair looks smooth. Apply additional joint compound should sanding expose any repair materials. Also apply additional joint compound should sanding compromise the shape or contour of the repair.

Non-flush repairs, because of their contour, will not be completely flat and uniform to the surface; flush-fill repairs should be flat and uniform to the surrounding surface. Non-flush repairs, when properly sanded, will **appear to be flush with the surrounding surface** when primed and painted. If your non-flush repair does not appear flush to the surface after priming, apply additional compound to restore the correct shape and contour.

For a review of sanding instruction, see the following sections:

SANDING, *on Pages 88-94*

HOW TO SAND NON-FLUSH SURFACE PREPARATION REPAIRS, *on Pages 113-114*

Repair of surfaces with plastic anchors and metal Molly bolt jackets

Plastic anchors and metal Molly bolts (all of which are called "fasteners") are installed into wall surfaces to provide a base into which a screw can be fastened that will support the weight of a picture, curtain rod, wall hanging or other decorative accessory. Fasteners have "arms" and casing parts that open and expand inside the wall upon installation. Once opened or expanded, the fastener is ready for load-bearing.

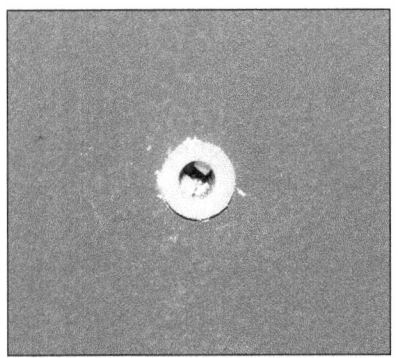

Figure 6.17
Plastic anchor.

Fasteners present a challenge in surface preparation, as installed fasteners can cause significant damage to the surface if forcibly removed. Occasionally, you may get lucky and be able to gently remove a plastic anchor or metal Molly bolt jacket from the surface with a pair of needle-nose pliers. In most cases, you will have to drive the fastener into, or though, the wall surface with a hammer.

Wall fastening devices other than those shown in *Figures 6.17 and 6.18* should not be dimpled or driven past the wall without first being inspected by a drywall contractor (for drywall surfaces) or a plasterer (for plaster surfaces). Some fastening devices may cause more damage should they be driven into the wall than they would by careful removal from the wall. Many of these devices are custom-made to hang heavy artworks, mirrors, or sectional glass pieces. Contact the manufacturer of custom-made hanging devices before attempting to remove them. **This repair method should only be used on the plastic anchors and metal Molly bolt jackets pictured in Figures 6.17 and 6.18.**

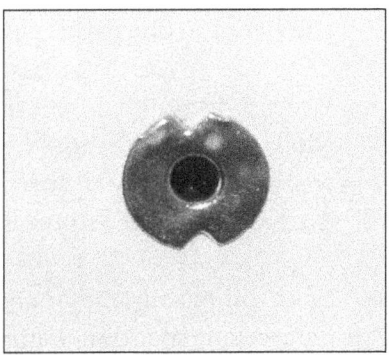

Figure 6.18
Metal Molly bolt jacket.

Safety Note: Consult with a licensed electrician before beginning this repair near an electrical outlet, switch or any electrical fixture.

Plaster surface note:

Using this repair method on plaster surfaces can result in plaster surface damage. Have a plasterer inspect all anchors, Molly bolt jackets and other fastening devices during the inspection of plaster surfaces. *(See Page 47)* Follow the advice of your plasterer concerning the repair of surfaces with plastic anchors, metal Molly bolt jackets, and all other fastening devices. For best results, a plasterer should be hired to complete these repairs. Allow curing of plaster repairs before the application of primer/sealer. *(See Page 101)*

Before beginning this repair: Warning for hammer use

Repairing surfaces with plastic anchors and metal Molly bolt jackets requires the use of a hammer. Before beginning this repair, see *Before beginning nail pop repair: Warning for hammer use*, on Page 124.

Tools and materials

Eye and respiratory system protection, work gloves, hammer, nail set, 6" taping knife, putty knife, mud tray and joint compound, lightweight spackling compound, fine/medium-grit sanding sponge, wiping cloth or towel, oil-based quick-drying primer/sealer, empty paint can, "all paints" paintbrush, 9" roller frame with ³/₈" nap cover, rolling pan, paint thinner and hand cleaner.

Steps

1. Wear eye and respiratory system protection. Work gloves should be worn to protect hands.
   (*See Pages 19-20 for eye and respiratory system protection information*)

2. Use a screwdriver or electric screwdriver to remove the screw from the anchor or Molly bolt jacket.

3. Sand the wall area around the anchor or Molly bolt jacket using the medium-grit side of a sanding sponge or 80-grit sandpaper.

4. Remove sanding dust with a wiping cloth or towel. Slightly dampening the wiping cloth or towel will help to control dust. Allow any surface moisture to dry before going to *Step 5*.

5. Using a drywall hammer or hammer, dimple a plastic anchor ¹/₈" below the surface. Metal Molly bolt jackets should be dimpled at least ¹/₄" below the surface, or hammered through the wall surface, (drywall surface) using a hammer and nail set. Rusted Molly bolt jackets should be driven through the drywall using a hammer and nail set.

6. Flush-fill plastic anchor and metal Molly bolt jacket dimples with drywall joint compound or lightweight spackling compound. Lightweight spackling compound should be used to flush-fill holes left when plastic anchors and metal Molly bolt jackets go through the wall. Allow drying.

7. Apply a second coat of the repair compound used in *Step 6*. Flush-fill. Allow drying. Apply a third coat of repair compound, if necessary. Allow drying.

8. Lightly sand the dried repair with the fine-grit side of a sanding sponge.

9. Remove sanding dust with a wiping cloth or towel. Slightly dampening the wiping cloth or towel will help to control dust. Allow any surface moisture to dry before going to *Step 10*.

10. Stir then pour oil-based quick-drying primer/sealer into an empty paint can. Two or three inches in the paint can will usually be enough to complete the cutting in of one ceiling or wall surface where dimple repairs are located.

    Apply a coat of oil-based quick-drying primer/sealer over the repair using either a slim roller frame and cover, or a 9" roller frame and ³/₈" nap roller cover. Allow drying.

    Note: If oil-based products are no longer available in your area, use a high-quality latex primer/sealer in this step. Follow directions for cleaning tools, hands and skin. Wear any recommended respiratory system protection.

    Note: If other preparation or repair work will be done, then apply primer/sealer in this room or part of the project after all preparation and repair work has been completed.

11. Lightly sand the dried primer/sealer with the fine-grit side of a sanding sponge. Entire ceiling and wall surfaces can be sanded using a pole sander with 100-grit or 120-grit pole sander paper.

    After sanding, remove sanding dust with a wiping cloth or towel. Slightly dampening the wiping cloth or towel will help to control dust. Allow any surface moisture to dry before going to *Step 12*.

12. Apply paint, decorative paint, faux finish or stencil.

Refer to Chapter 1 for information regarding safety and avoiding spontaneous combustion fire when using paint thinner, turpentine, mineral spirits, denatured alcohol, paint deglosser, oil-based primers and primer/sealers and White-Pigmented Shellac.

Estimated Time to Complete this Technique

The estimated time to complete the repair of a plastic anchor or metal Molly bolt jacket is one day. The actual working time to complete the repair will be approximately twenty minutes.

Note: Estimated time to complete method steps includes drying times for repair compounds and primer/sealer. Refer to the directions on the container for drying times of repair compounds and primer/sealer. Humid conditions will lengthen drying times. Other preparation and repair work can be done in the room while waiting for repair compounds to dry.

Tips and Troubleshooting

Repair of surfaces with plastic anchors and metal Molly bolt jackets

Avoid excessive hammering, or "over-dimpling," of plastic anchors. Excessive hammering causes deep dimples that require additional coats of drywall joint compound to flush-fill. It may also cause drywall cover damage.

SUPPORTING CRACKED CEILING DRYWALL AND REFASTENING SAGGING CEILING DRYWALL

Crack repair on ceilings often fails when the drywall around the crack is sagging, or poorly fastened. A noticeable accumulation of applied drywall joint compound with a crack near the center is a reliable indicator of one or more failed ceiling crack repairs. If an inadequate number or drywall screws or drywall nails were used to fasten ceiling drywall during installation, cracking and sagging may result. Age, and the expansion and contraction of surfaces caused by seasonal temperature variation, can also cause drywall surfaces to crack and sag.

Ceiling crack repairs are more likely to succeed when the drywall around the crack is supported with additional drywall nails or drywall screws before crack repair begins. Refastening sagging ceiling drywall helps to keep drywall from cracking due to stress on poorly-fastened areas. See *Table 6.2* for indicators of sagging ceiling drywall.

Before beginning this repair: Warning for hammer use

When drywall nails are used in this repair, the use of a drywall hammer or claw hammer is required. Before beginning this repair, see *Before beginning nail pop repair: Warning for hammer use*, on Page 124.

Notes:
In some instances, cracked and/or sagging drywall will need to be replaced. Whenever you have concern regarding the soundness or repairability of a drywall surface, seek the advice of a licensed professional drywall contractor.

DO NOT attempt this repair on plaster ceilings.

Indicators of sagging ceiling drywall

Nail pops
Nail pops result from a loosening of nails that support drywall. Drywall my have begun to sag where nail pops are present. *(See REPAIRING DRYWALL NAIL POPS, on Page 124)*

Ceiling cracks
Ceiling cracks indicate the possible location of sagging drywall.

Visible sagging between ceiling joists
Sagging ceiling drywall is often visible between adjacent ceiling joists. Late afternoon and early evening sunlight offer an excellent opportunity to visually check for ceiling drywall sagging.

Table 6.2

Chapter 6 Common Surface Preparation Repairs

Tools and materials

Eye and respiratory system protection, drill driver with magnetic drive guide and 1³/₈" drywall screws or hammer or drywall hammer and ringed drywall nails, stud finder, pencil, joint compound, mud tray, 6" taping knife, fine/medium-grit sanding sponge, wiping cloth or towel, "all paints" paintbrush, empty paint can, oil-based primer/sealer, 9" roller frame with ³/₈" nap roller cover, extension rolling pole, rolling pan, paint thinner and hand cleaner.

Steps

1. Wear eye and respiratory system protection.
   (*See Pages 19-20 for eye and respiratory system protection information*)

2. Locate ceiling joists in the cracking or sagging area with an electronic or magnetic stud finder. Make light pencil marks to identify the location of ceiling joists along the area of sagging and/or cracked drywall.

3. In this step, use a pencil to mark locations along the ceiling joists to drive drywall screws, or hammer ringed drywall nails.

Where drywall has cracked:

Along the first joist, make your first set of pencil marks an inch from the crack. (one on each side of the crack) Make another set of marks six inches on either side of your first marks. Finish by making another set of marks six inches on either side of the last marks. You should now have marks on either side of the crack at 1", 7" and 13." *(Figure 6.19, below)* If the drywall is sagging past the 13" marks, then continue making a set of marks every twelve inches until all the sagging drywall has been marked. Repeat this process along each joist the crack passes. As a preventative measure for cracks that extend for only a few joists (up to four or five), refasten drywall one ceiling joist past the crack on each end of the crack. *(Figure 6.20, on next page)* This extra support may help to prevent the crack from lengthening.

Figure 6.19
Supporting the ceiling drywall around a crack with drywall screws.
This photo shows the screws driven into one ceiling joist.

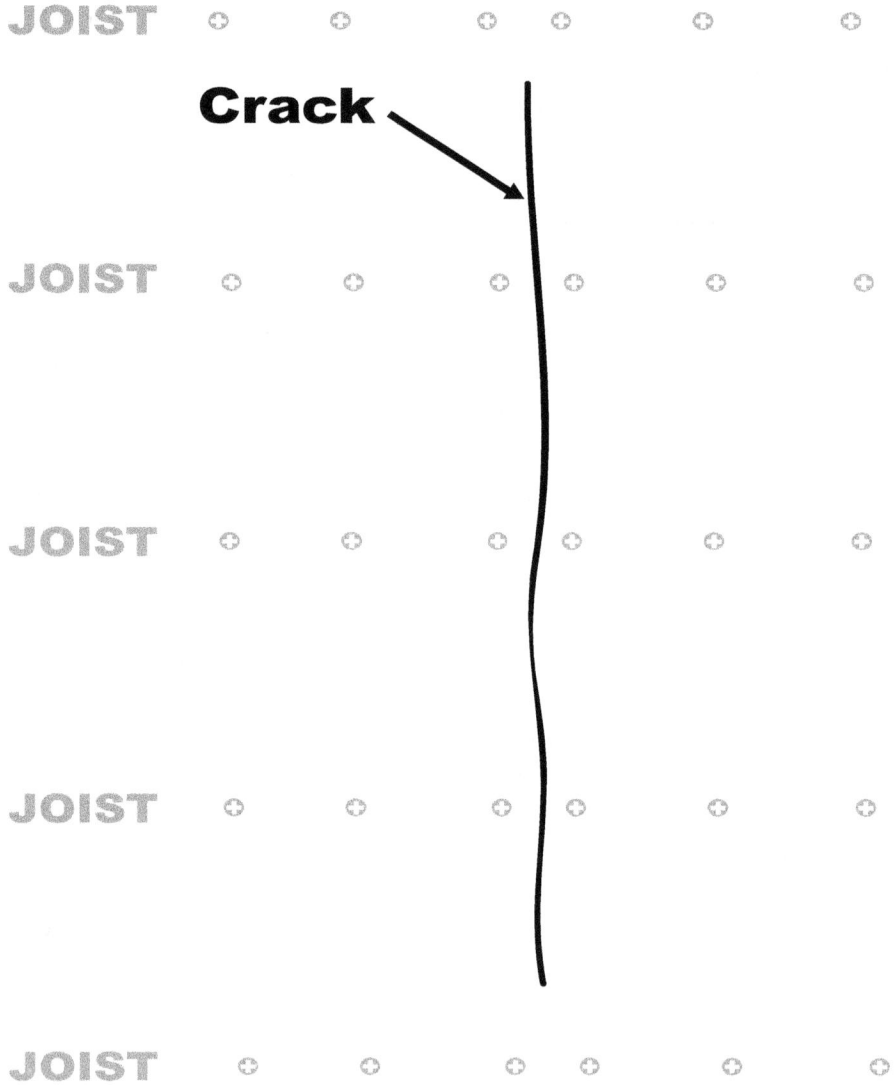

Figure 6.20
This diagram shows an expanded view of the area in *Figure 6.19, on previous page*. The drywall around the crack has been supported by additional screws. The repair continues one joist past each end of the crack. After the drywall around the crack has been supported, begin crack repair.

For cracks already half-way, or more, across the ceiling, you may be wise to refasten drywall on each ceiling joist in the room or area along the "projected path" (direction the crack looks to be spreading) of the crack. Supporting the drywall across the ceiling will help to prevent the crack from spreading, which may save you from having to repair the crack in the future.

Where drywall is sagging without cracking:

Make a mark every twelve inches along each ceiling joist where the sagging is located. As a preventative measure, make your last twelve-inch mark in an area that is not sagging. It is also a good idea to mark and refasten drywall one ceiling joist to the left and right of sagging areas. The extra support will help to keep the drywall from sagging around the perimeter of the repair.

4. Use a drill driver with a magnetic drive guide, or drywall dimple bit, to fasten drywall with 1 3/8" drywall screws at your pencil marks. Drive screws just below the surface of the drywall. If the drywall screws are difficult to drive just below the surface, then use 1¼" drywall screws. If you are using ringed drywall nails, drive them with a drywall hammer, or hammer, just below the surface creating a dimple.
   Note: If you are hammering ringed drywall nails in this step, a drywall hammer is a better tool choice than a regular hammer.

5. Use a 6" taping knife to apply joint compound to flush-fill the area over driven screws, or nail dimples. Allow drying.

6. Apply a second coat of joint compound. Allow drying.

7. Apply a third coat of joint compound, if necessary. Allow drying.

8. Sand the dried joint compound with the fine-grit side of a sanding sponge.

9. Remove sanding dust with a wiping cloth or towel. Slightly dampening the wiping cloth or towel will help to control dust. Allow any surface moisture to dry before going to *Step 10*.

10. Stir then pour oil-based quick-drying primer/sealer into an empty paint can. Two or three inches in the paint can will usually be enough to complete the cutting in of one ceiling or wall surface where repairs are located. Apply a coat of oil-based quick-drying primer/sealer over the repaired surface using a 9" roller frame, 3/8" nap roller cover and extension rolling pole. Allow drying.
    Note: If oil-based products are no longer available in your area, use a high-quality latex primer/sealer in this step. Follow directions for cleaning tools, hands and skin. Wear recommended respiratory system protection.
    Note: If other preparation or repair work will be done, then apply primer/sealer in this room or part of the project after all preparation and repair work has been completed.

11. Lightly sand the dried primer/sealer with the fine-grit side of a sanding sponge. Larger areas can be sanded using a pole sander with 100-grit or 120-grit pole sander paper.

    Remove sanding dust with a wiping cloth or towel. Slightly dampening the wiping cloth or towel will help to control dust. Allow any surface moisture to dry before going to *Step 12*.

12. Apply paint, decorative paint, faux finish or stencil.

Refer to Chapter 1 for information regarding safety and avoiding spontaneous combustion fire when using paint thinner, turpentine, mineral spirits, denatured alcohol, paint deglosser, oil-based primers and primer/sealers and White-Pigmented Shellac.

Estimated Time to Complete this Technique

The estimated time to complete this repair can range from one to several hours. In rooms where drywall must be supported or refastened in several locations, a day or more may be required.

Note: Estimated time to complete method steps includes drying times for repair compounds and primer/sealer. Refer to the directions on the container for drying times of repair compounds and primer/sealer. Humid conditions will lengthen drying times. Other preparation and repair work can be done in the room while waiting for repair compounds to dry.

TIPS AND TROUBLESHOOTING

Supporting cracked ceiling drywall and refastening sagging ceiling drywall

1. It is better to drive a few extra nails or screws than not enough.

2. If a drywall screw can not be driven just below the surface, back it out and try a slightly shorter screw. If that does not work, then drive the screw into another area along the joist that is close to your mark.

3. Visually inspect the ceiling after supporting areas of cracked or sagging drywall. After repairs are completed in one area, drywall nails may pop (in other areas of the ceiling) as a result of the repair. *(See REPAIRING DRYWALL NAIL POPS, on Page 124)*

REPAIRING CRACKS

Crack repair is a common surface preparation task. Both drywall and plaster surfaces are prone to cracking as homes age and settle. You will likely need to complete at least one crack repair in almost every room you are preparing for paint, decorative paint, faux finish or stencils.

The crack repair method covered in this book can be used on both drywall and the white coat layer of plaster surfaces. It uses self-adhesive mesh drywall joint tape and drywall joint compound.

Plaster surface note: A licensed professional plasterer should inspect plaster surfaces before surface preparation work begins. *(See Page 47)*

Drywall ceiling note: Before beginning crack repair on a drywall ceiling, be sure to have read the previous section: Supporting cracked ceiling drywall and refastening sagging ceiling drywall.

Crack repair basics

Location

Cracks can often be found in the header area above doors and windows. *(Figures 6.21 and 6.22)* Most header cracks are located towards the end of a header. A crack at the end of a header usually extends up from the corner area of the trim. *(Figure 6.22)* Cracks found at the end of a header are often the widest and deepest that you will have to repair. They are also the cracks that are most likely to re-appear and need later repair.

Also look for cracks in ceilings, corners and below windows.

Why loose material must be removed

It is important to remove all loose material over, around, and in the crack, as loose material may prevent the durable adhesion of repair materials.

On drywall surfaces, such loose material may include drywall joint tape, dried drywall joint compound, and bits of cracked or peeling paint.

Figure 6.21
Door header crack.

On plaster surfaces, such loose material may include drywall joint tape, dried joint compound, and paint that has cracked or peeled. It may also include small bits, or granules, of plaster.

Scoring an inverted "V"

An inverted "V" is scored within the crack to remove all loose material from the crack, and the area bordering the crack. This is done by using the corner of the blade of a rigid-blade putty knife or scraper. *(Figure 6.22)*

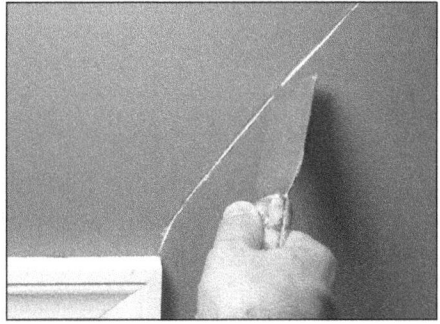

Figure 6.22
Loosen and remove unstable material from the crack using a putty knife or scraper.

Door header crack pictured. This crack is located near the end of a header.

Make the inverted "V"-shape score inside the crack by running the corner of the putty knife or scraper blade along each side of the crack, and then down the middle of the crack. The tip of your putty knife or scraper blade should then be used to scrape flat over the top of the crack. If material is loosened by scraping flat over the top of the crack, then run the corner of the blade back down the sides and center of the crack again. These motions will loosen and remove any unstable material from within and around the crack. The removal of loose material will create the inverted "V" shape. *(Figure 6.23)*

In some instances, the surface around the crack will be stable, and only a slight inverted "V" will result after scoring strokes. *(Figure 6.23)* This is fine. Once any loose material has been removed, there is no need to continue applying force to remove stable material from within, around and over the crack. *(See Ambulance Box, on next page)*

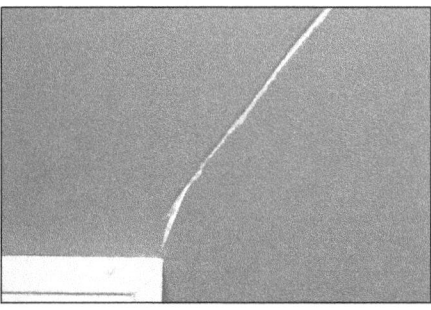

Figure 6.23
Scored inverted "V." Surface is sanded around the crack.

In drywall surfaces, an inverted "V"-shape score can often be achieved with just a few light strokes to the left-side, right-side, center and border area over the crack.

In plaster surfaces, an inverted "V"-shape may require several strokes to each side, the middle, and border area over the top of the crack. The inverted "V" will usually be more pronounced in plaster surface cracks than drywall cracks.

Note: Consult a licensed professional plasterer should scoring strokes cause cracking in, or lead to the removal of, any piece of the plaster white coat layer. (other than small granules)

Do not use excessive force in attempting to score an inverted "V" on drywall or plaster surfaces. If material is loose within and around the crack, it can be removed by using light, even pressure. ***Excessive force can lead to personal injury and damage to tools and surfaces.***

Scrapers and putty knives have metal blades that can cause cuts and injury. Wearing work gloves will help to protect your hands when using a putty knife or scraper to remove material over, around, and within a crack.

Self-adhesive mesh drywall joint tape

The crack repair method covered in this book uses self-adhesive mesh drywall joint tape. *(Figure 6.24)* This genre of joint tape, manufactured by many companies, combines a strong, open, fiberglass mesh with an adhesive backing. The open mesh enables easy filling (of the mesh) with drywall joint compound. It also adds strength to the repair. The adhesive backing provides secure fastening to the surface without the need to "set" the tape into a bed (coat) of drywall joint compound, a requirement of using paper drywall joint tape.

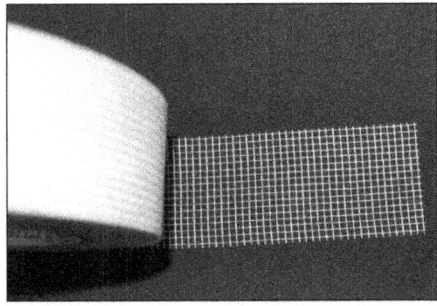

Figure 6.24
Roll of self-adhesive mesh tape.

Another big advantage of using self-adhesive mesh tape is that it is more forgiving than paper drywall joint tape. If you do not properly set paper joint tape into a bed of evenly-applied joint compound, then your paper tape may not adequately adhere to the surface. Areas of paper joint tape that do not adhere well to the surface often lift at the edges, and/or bubble within the borders of the tape. (bubbled areas are also called "blisters") Areas of the tape that have lifted or bubbled need to be removed, and then re-taped.

For beginners, self-adhesive mesh drywall joint tape is much easier to install than paper joint tape, and the achievement of consistently-good results is more readily attainable.

Paper drywall joint tape

As mentioned in the section above, paper drywall joint tape can be difficult for a beginner to use. For that reason, this book does not include a crack repair method using paper drywall joint tape.

Applying decorative paint, faux finish, mural art or stencils over drywall or plaster surfaces that have cracks

Crack repair, especially in the header areas above doors and windows, may have to be repeated every few years as structures move and settle. For best results, locate your decorative painted finish, faux finish, mural art or stencils on drywall or plaster surfaces that have a minimum of cracking, or no cracking at all.

REPAIRING CRACKS WITH SELF-ADHESIVE MESH DRYWALL JOINT TAPE AND DRYWALL JOINT COMPOUND

This method of crack repair uses self-adhesive mesh drywall joint tape, also called "mesh tape," and drywall joint compound.

Tools and materials

Eye and respiratory system protection, 6" taping knife, putty knife, mud tray and joint compound, self-adhesive mesh drywall joint tape, scissors, fine/medium-grit sanding sponge, wiping cloth or towel, oil-based quick-drying primer/sealer, empty paint can, "all paints" paintbrush, 9" roller frame with ³⁄₈" nap cover and extension rolling pole, rolling pan, paint thinner and hand cleaner.

Steps

1. Wear eye and respiratory system protection. (*See Pages 19-20 for eye and respiratory system protection information*)

2. Use a rigid blade putty knife or scraper to remove any loose material that is over the crack. Gently pry the edges or ends of any loose joint tape. *(Figure 6.26)* Remove loose joint tape, and then square the end, or ends, of any remaining tape (still solidly in place) with a utility knife. *(Figures 6.27-6.29)*

3. Use the corner of the putty knife or scraper blade to score an inverted "V" along the inside of the crack. *(Figure 6.30, on opposite page and Figure 6.22, on Page 141)* Make the inverted "V" by running the corner of the putty knife or scraper blade along each side and down the middle of the crack. *(Figure 6.23, on Page 141)* Then use the tip of your putty knife or scraper blade to scrape flat over the top of the crack. If scraping over the top removes any material, then rescore the left-side, right-side and center of the crack again. These motions will loosen any unstable material from within and around the crack. Remove all material loosened by this process.

4. Sand the repair surface with the medium-grit side of a sanding sponge or 80-grit sandpaper. *(Figure 6.32)* Then use a duster to remove sanding dust and loose debris. *(Figure 6.33)*

Figure 6.25
Self-adhesive mesh drywall joint tape, drywall joint compound in mud tray, putty knife and 6" taping knife.

Figures 6.26, 6.27
Remove loose material with a rigid blade putty knife or scraper. Any loosened drywall joint tape should also be removed.

5. Use scissors to cut enough self-adhesive mesh tape to cover the length of the crack plus two inches on each end, when possible. (An extra two inches is not necessary when joint tape is applied up to a squared end of tape, as would be the case in *Figure 6.29*) The extra length of tape should be applied in the direction of the crack. This preventative measure helps to keep the crack covered should it continue to spread. Center the mesh tape over the crack, gently pressing to bond the adhesive side to the repair surface. Use fingertips to press mesh tape into corners, as using a putty knife or taping knife can split the tape. Cut the mesh tape into smaller pieces and center it over the crack should the crack changes directions. Some overlapping of mesh tape is acceptable. Use a utility knife to cut any portion of the mesh tape that bubbles or does not lie flat. This cut is similar to a relief cut when installing wallpaper. *(See Making a relief cut to smooth a mesh tape bubble, on Page 150)*

6. Apply joint compound over and just beyond the mesh tape using a 6" taping knife. Remove excess compound. The mesh should be filled but still visible after the first coat. Allow drying.

Figure 6.28
Removing loosened paper joint tape.

Figure 6.29
Using a utility knife to square the end of remaining joint tape.

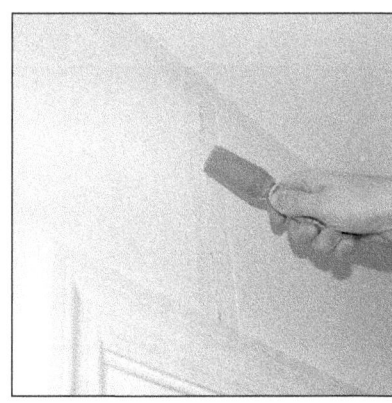

Figure 6.30
Removing loose material from the crack.

Figure 6.31
Inverted "V" scored in a similar door header crack.

Figure 6.32
Sanding the area around the crack.

Figure 6.33
Using a duster to remove sanding dust and loose debris.

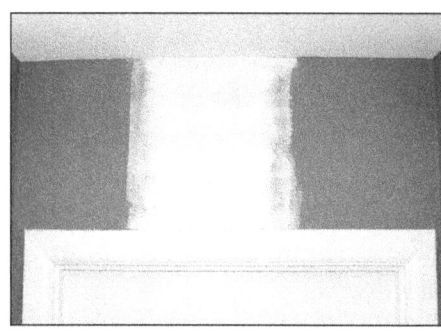

Figure 6.34
Door header crack repair (similar to the examples on the previous two pages) after three coats of drywall joint compound. The applied compound has a flat top with contoured edges to the left and right of the crack. Application measures fourteen-inches across.

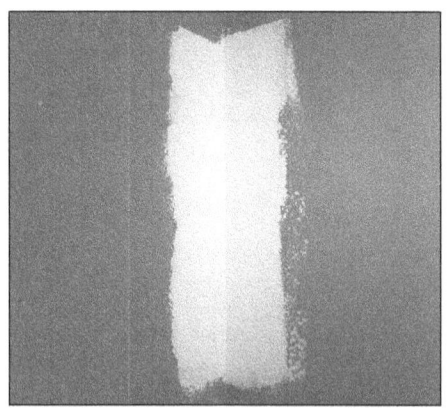

Figure 6.35
Inside corner crack repair after three coats of joint compound. Application extends four inches on each side of the crack.

Joint compound application tip:

For the second and third coats, apply joint compound to only one side of the repair at a time, extending the application into the corner. After drying, apply compound to the other side of the repair, extending the application into the corner. Finishing strokes with the taping knife should be from the top of the application to the bottom, with a slight contour on the edges. Repeat for the third coat. This technique will help you to make a good inside corner.

7. Apply a second coat of joint compound over mesh tape, extending the application approximately two inches beyond the border of the first application. For corners, extend the second application approximately one-and-a-half inches.

   For crack repairs on a wall or ceiling, make an oval-shaped joint compound application with contoured edges. After the second coat, the repair should begin to resemble *Figure 6.36.*

   For crack repairs that extend the full length of a wall or ceiling, make a rectangular-shaped application with contoured edges. After the second coat, the repair should begin to resemble *Figure 6.34.*

   For crack repairs that extend to a wall corner, ceiling corner, or piece of trim, making an oval-shaped application is not necessary. In these instances, make a rectangular-shaped application of joint compound with contoured edges as seen in *Figure 6.34.* Should the other end of the crack repair stop before reaching a corner or piece of trim, then apply joint compound on that end using an oval-shaped arc.

   For crack repairs over a header, *(Figure 6.34)* make a rectangular-shaped application with contoured edges. After the second coat, the repair should begin to resemble *Figure 6.34.*

   For crack repairs at the end of a header, *(Figure 6.23, on Page 141)*, make an oval-shaped joint compound application with contoured edges. After the second coat, the repair should begin to resemble *Figure 6.37.*

   For crack repairs in corners, make a rectangular-shaped application with contoured edges on each side of the corner. After the second coat, the repair should begin to resemble *Figure 6.35.*

   If you need to review how to shape and contour repairs, *turn back to Page 110.*

8. Allow drying.

9. Repeat *Step 7* when applying a third coat of joint compound. Allow drying. The mesh should be completely covered after the third coat of joint compound. Apply a fourth coat of joint compound if the mesh tape is visible, or if the repair is not properly shaped or contoured. Only a partial coat may be needed. Allow drying.

10. Use the fine-grit side of a sanding sponge to sand the repair. If sanding exposes any mesh tape, apply joint compound. Sand when dry.

    If you need to review how to sand non-flush repairs, *turn back to Page 113.*

11. Remove sanding dust with a wiping cloth or towel. Slightly dampening the wiping cloth or towel will help to control dust. Allow any surface moisture to dry before going to *Step 12.*

Figure 6.36
Horizontal crack repair after the fourth coat of joint compound. The completed repair extended five inches above and below the mesh tape. It also extended five inches past the ends of the tape.

12. Stir then pour oil-based quick-drying primer/sealer into an empty paint can. Two or three inches in the paint can will usually be enough to complete the cutting in of one ceiling or wall surface where crack repairs are located. Apply a coat of oil-based quick-drying primer/sealer over the repaired surface using a slim roller frame and cover, or a 9" roller frame, 3/8" nap roller cover and extension rolling pole. Allow drying.

    Note: If oil-based products are no longer available in your area, use a high-quality latex primer/sealer in this step. Follow directions for cleaning tools, hands and skin. Wear any recommended respiratory system protection.

    Note: If other preparation or repair work will be done, then apply primer/sealer in this room or part of the project after all preparation and repair work has been completed.

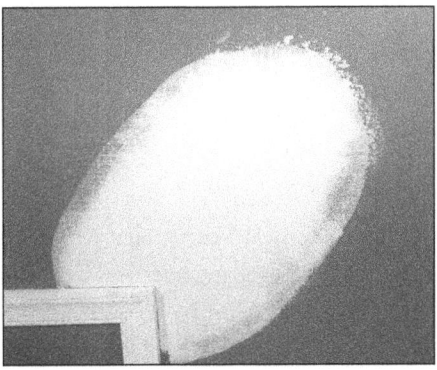

Figure 6.37
Crack repair covered by three coats of joint compound. Applied joint compound measures approximately twelve inches across the width of the repair.

13. Lightly sand the dried primer/sealer with the fine-grit side of a sanding sponge. Large ceiling and wall areas can be sanded using a pole sander with 100-grit or 120-grit pole sander paper.

14. Remove sanding dust with a wiping cloth or towel. Slightly dampening the wiping cloth or towel will help to control dust. Allow any surface moisture to dry before going to *Step 15.*

15. Apply paint, decorative paint, faux finish or stencil.

Refer to Chapter 1 for information regarding safety and avoiding spontaneous combustion fire when using paint thinner, turpentine, mineral spirits, denatured alcohol, paint deglosser, oil-based primers and primer/sealers and White-Pigmented Shellac.

Estimated Time to Complete this Technique

The estimated time to complete a crack repair of approximately twelve inches is one day. The actual working time will be approximately thirty minutes.

Note: Estimated time to complete steps includes drying times for repair compounds and primer/sealer. Refer to the directions on the container for drying times of repair compounds and primer/sealer. Humid conditions will lengthen drying times. Other preparation and repair work can be done in the room while waiting for repair compounds to dry.

TIPS AND TROUBLESHOOTING

Crack repair using self-adhesive mesh drywall joint tape and drywall joint compound

1. To avoid difficulty finding the end of the mesh tape on the roll after cutting, bend the tape before cutting, and make your cut just above the bend. *(See* **Crease self-adhesive mesh tape to keep track of the end,** *on next page)*

2. Use a utility knife to cut any strands of mesh that become separated from the rest of the tape. Separated strands are often located on the edges or ends of the mesh tape. They often become separated during contact with the taping knife during the application of joint compound.

3. Crack repair that is done over the noticeable accumulation of joint compound from previous repairs can be difficult to conceal. To help hide the repair, you may need to apply extra coats of joint compound. In some instances, you may need eight-inches, or more, of application on either side of the mesh tape. Once mesh tape is covered, avoid making the repair thicker, and work to distribute the existing height, or thickness, of the repair over a wider area. Extend (widen) the application until you see more acceptable results.

   Try using a flexible blade eight-inch taping knife for wide joint compound applications.

TIPS FOR WORKING WITH SELF-ADHESIVE MESH DRYWALL JOINT TAPE

In the last section, you were introduced to self-adhesive mesh drywall joint tape in the crack repair method. Its strong, open, fiberglass mesh design, and adhesive backing, make it the ideal joint tape for beginning surface preparation students. Although easy to use, there are a few tips that I can illustrate in this section that will help you to work more efficiently with mesh tape.

Crease self-adhesive mesh tape to keep track of the end

It is very easy to loose track of the end of the self-adhesive mesh tape roll. When a length of tape is cut, the end will often fasten itself back onto the roll. When this occurs, the end can be difficult to locate. It can also be difficult to lift when another piece of mesh tape is needed. The time lost trying to locate and lift the end of the tape is time that can be put to better use.

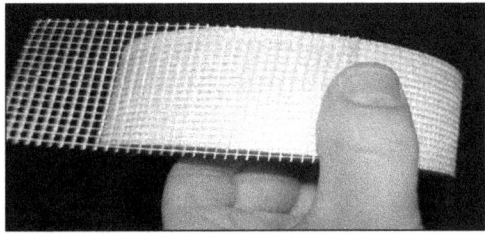

Figure 6.38
Bending the mesh tape to create a crease.

This three-step method will help you to easily keep track of the roll's end:

1. Measure the length of self-adhesive mesh drywall joint tape that you need, and then add an extra ¼" to ⅜."

2. At the measured point that includes the extra amount, use your thumb to bend the tape back against the roll to create a crease. *(Figure 6.38)* Some may find it easier to use both thumbs to create the crease.

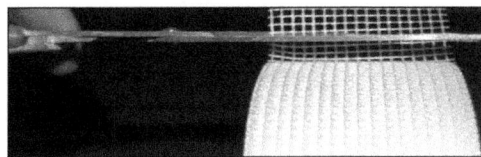

Figure 6.39
Cutting mesh tape above the crease to create a "tab."

3. Use scissors to cut the mesh tape ¼" to ⅜" above the crease. *(Figure 6.39)* Once cut, the extra ¼" to ⅜" of mesh tape above the crease becomes a raised tab that can be easily found, and grasped. *(Figure 6.40)*

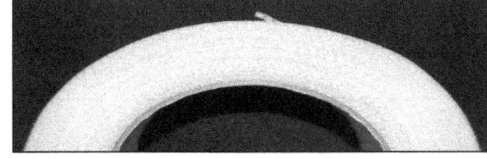

Figure 6.40
End of the mesh tape roll is now a raised tab ready for the next length to be cut.

For best results, use a pair of sharp scissors to cut mesh tape. Scissors make the cleanest cut on mesh tape, which is important as a clean cut helps to keep the strands of mesh intact. (keeps them from separating from the tape) A utility knife can also be used to cut mesh tape, but you will likely find that scissors work best.

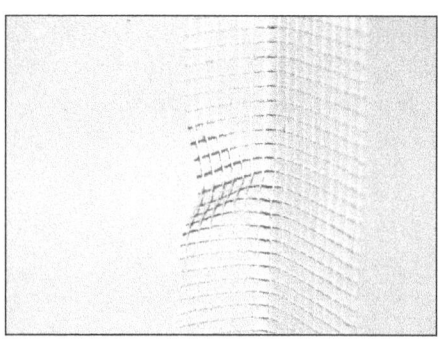

Figure 6.41
Self-adhesive mesh drywall joint tape bubble.

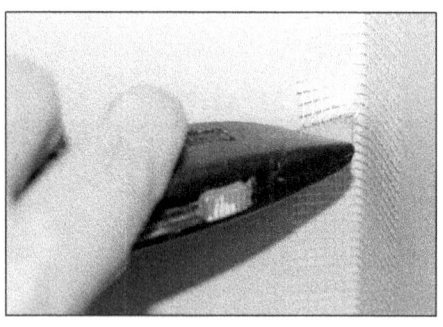

Figure 6.42
Cutting the bubble with a utility knife.

Figure 6.43
Cut ends after they have been pressed down to the surface.

Making a relief cut to smooth a mesh tape bubble

Mesh tape may bubble when applied over an irregular surface. The most common occurrence of a mesh tape bubble can often be found where mesh tape is applied into an inside corner that is somewhat out of square. *(Figure 6.41)* Regardless of where a mesh tape bubble occurs, it should be removed before the application of drywall joint compound.

In some cases, a mesh tape bubble can be eliminated by simply removing the mesh tape and placing it back on the surface. This is the easiest remedy and should be tried a time or two before other action is taken.

If the bubble still can not be removed, then a relief cut should be made. The term "relief cut" comes from the installation of wallpaper. In general terms, a relief cut is made so that wallpaper will lie flat. As our objective is to have the mesh tape lie flat, we will employ the relief cut technique.

This relief cut technique will help you to eliminate mesh tape bubbles:

1. Center the utility knife blade over the bubbled area and cut the tape. Work from the corner out. *(Figure 6.42)*

2. Use fingers to gently press the cut ends down to the surface. You will likely have to overlap one end over the other.

For best results, have a fresh blade in your utility knife when cutting mesh tape. If cutting mesh tape results in a flyaway, (strand of the tape that pulls away from the rest) remove the flyaway strand, or strands, by cutting with the utility knife. Having a fresh blade in your utility knife will help to reduce the chances of causing a flyaway strand.

Cutting self-adhesive mesh drywall joint tape along its length

Although most mesh tape cuts are made across the width, mesh tape can also be cut along its length. The length-wise cut provides the amount (width) of tape needed for crack repairs in narrow and confined areas, where a full width of mesh tape (approximately two inches) may be difficult to install and finish with drywall joint compound. In many cases, cutting the tape in-half length-wise will be beneficial for enabling crack repairs on wall surfaces where only two inches (give or take a little) of width exists between door or window trim, and a wall corner.

Narrow and confined-area crack repairs may be in corners, or on the wall surface between the corner and the nearby trim wood.

For best results, use scissors to make a length-wise cut.

Figure 6.44
Torn drywall cover damage exposing brown paper layers beneath the cover.

REPAIRING DRYWALL COVER DAMAGE

Damage to the drywall cover is often caused by either the removal of a glued or adhesive-backed item, or an object that collides with the drywall surface. Removal of wallpaper, borders, masking tape, stickers, and other glued or adhesive-backed items, will often tear, and sometimes remove, portions of the drywall cover. Furniture, and any other object that comes in contact with drywall, may also scuff or tear the cover.

Damage that tears the drywall cover often exposes the brown paper layers beneath the cover. *(See Figure 6.44)* The brown paper layers are thin and often separate, or blister, when exposed to the moisture of applied repair compounds and paint.

Correct repair of drywall cover damage helps to prevent greater surface preparation problems later.

Note: Where severe or extensive drywall cover damage exists, it may be necessary to replace drywall. Consult with a licensed drywall contractor whenever you have concern about the soundness or repairability of a drywall surface.

Tools and materials

Eye and respiratory system protection, 6" taping knife, putty knife, self-adhesive mesh drywall joint tape, mud tray and drywall joint compound, fine/medium-grit sanding sponge, scissors, utility knife, wiping cloth or towel, oil-based quick-drying primer/sealer, empty paint can, "all paints" paintbrush, 9" roller frame with ³⁄₈" nap cover and extension rolling pole, rolling pan, paint thinner and hand cleaner.

Steps

1. Wear eye and respiratory system protection. *(See Pages 19-20 for eye and respiratory system protection information)*

2. Remove any torn pieces of drywall cover and any torn, or bubbled, brown paper using a utility knife. Also cut and remove any raised cover edges bordering damaged areas. Damaged areas should be left with secure (unraised) edges and no loose or bubbled brown paper or material. *(See inset picture at the top-left of Figure 6.45, on opposite page)*

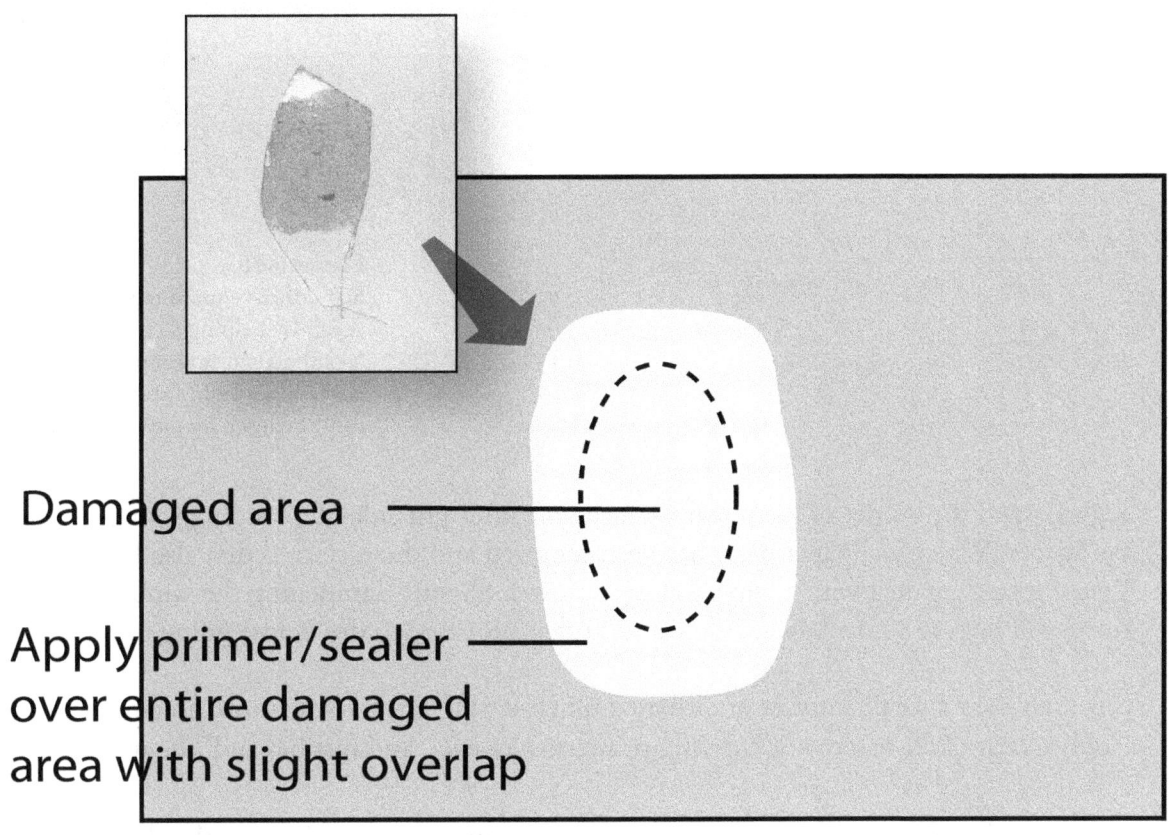

Figure 6.45
Oil-based quick-drying primer/sealer stiffens cover edges and exposed brown paper layers. It also seals the repair, helping to prevent further damage by protecting against moisture from applied joint compound and paint.

Inset picture top-left shows Figure 6.44 after the removal of the torn cover piece as mentioned in *Step 2*. The scratches below the exposed brown paper should be considered part of the damaged area and coated with primer/sealer.

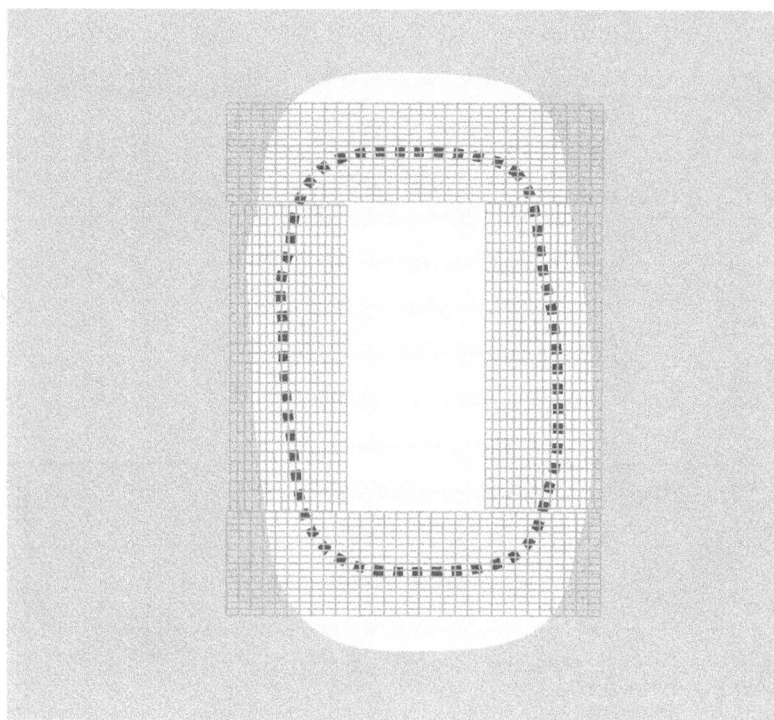

Figure 6.46
Self-adhesive mesh tape strengthens the repair by helping to hold the damaged area together. It also protects the torn cover edges from further damage that can be caused by taping knife contact.

Lightly sand the border of the repair with the medium-grit side of a sanding sponge, or 80-grit sandpaper. Where wallpaper paste has been removed and the surface is dry, also lightly sand. Remove sanding dust with a wiping cloth or towel. Slightly dampening the wiping cloth or towel will help to control dust. Allow any surface moisture to dry before going to *Step 3*.

3. Stir then pour a small amount of oil-based quick-drying primer/sealer into an empty paint can. Apply a coat of oil-based quick-drying primer/sealer over, and just beyond, the damaged area. *(Fig. 6.45, on previous page)*

    Note: If oil-based products are no longer available in your area, use a high-quality latex drywall sealer capable of sealing down damaged drywall in this step.

4. Allow drying.

5. Use scissors to cut pieces of self-adhesive mesh drywall joint tape to cover all torn drywall cover edges. Center the mesh tape over the edges and press to bond the tape to the surface. *(Fig. 6.46)* Smaller repairs can be completely covered with mesh tape. *(Fig. 6.47, on opposite page)*

    Note: For damage caused by wallpaper or border removal, it is not necessary to cover all slightly torn or scuffed edges with self-adhesive mesh tape. In fact, if a good job was done in *Steps 2 and 3***, only a few, if any, damaged areas may require this step. Apply mesh tape in cases of severe tearing, such as a large area tear, or area that appears to have a pronounced edge after priming. When in doubt, apply mesh tape. It may be better to apply a little extra tape, than too little tape.**

6. Use a 6" taping knife to apply a coat of drywall joint compound over the repair area. The mesh should be filled but the tape should still visible after the first coat.

7. Allow drying. Joint compound is dry when uniformly white.

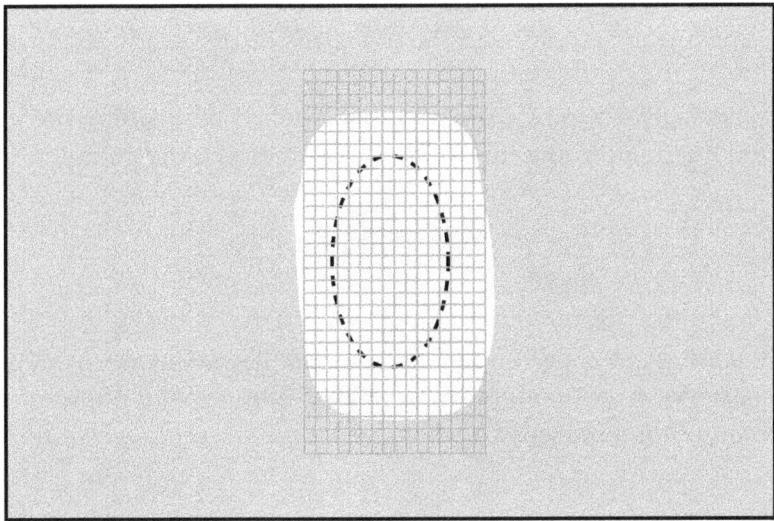

Figure 6.47
Entire damaged area covered with primer/sealer and self-adhesive mesh drywall joint tape. Mesh tape does not need to cover all of the primer/sealer application.

8. Apply a second coat of joint compound in a circular or oval shape extending approximately two inches past the first application. Use the 6" taping knife to properly contour the application. The joint compound application should be thinnest at the edges. It should begin to dry in just a few minutes. Allow drying.

9. Apply a third coat of joint compound using the same technique as in *Step 8*. The repair should now be concealed. Allow drying. Apply a fourth coat of joint compound if any area of the mesh tape is visible. A partial coat may be sufficient to cover small areas of exposed mesh tape. Allow drying.

10. Use the fine-grit side of a sanding sponge to sand the repair.

11. Remove sanding dust with a wiping cloth or towel. Slightly dampening the wiping cloth or towel will help to control dust. Allow any surface moisture to dry before going to *Step 12*.

12. Stir then pour oil-based quick-drying primer/sealer into an empty paint can. Two or three inches in the paint can will usually be enough to complete the cutting in of one ceiling or wall surface where drywall cover repairs have been completed. Apply a coat of oil-based quick-drying primer/sealer over the repaired surface using a 9" roller frame, 3/8" nap roller cover and extension rolling pole. A slim roller frame and cover or paintbrush can be used to apply primer/sealer over smaller repairs. Allow drying.

Note: If oil-based products are no longer available in your area, use a high-quality latex primer/sealer in this step. Follow directions for cleaning tools, hands and skin. Wear any recommended respiratory system protection.

Note: If other preparation or repair work will be done, then apply primer/sealer in this room or part of the project after all preparation and repair work has been completed.

13. Lightly sand the dried primer/sealer with the fine-grit side of a sanding sponge.

14. Remove sanding dust with a wiping cloth or towel. Slightly dampening the wiping cloth or towel will help to control dust. Allow any surface moisture to dry before going to *Step 15*.

15. Apply paint, decorative paint, faux finish or stencil.

Refer to Chapter 1 for information regarding safety and avoiding spontaneous combustion fire when using paint thinner, turpentine, mineral spirits, denatured alcohol, paint deglosser, oil-based primers and primer/sealers and White-Pigmented Shellac.

Estimated Time to Complete this Technique

The estimated time to complete the repair of a drywall cover tear is between one and two days. The actual working time to complete the repair of a drywall cover tear of two or three inches is approximately thirty minutes.

Note: Estimated time to complete steps includes drying times for repair compounds and primer/sealer. Refer to the directions on the container for drying times of repair compounds and primer/sealer. Humid conditions will lengthen drying times. Other preparation and repair work can be done in the room while waiting for repair compounds to dry.

Tips and Troubleshooting

Repairing drywall cover damage

1. After the oil-based primer/sealer has dried in *Step 4*, check the repair for any areas of bubbled or lifted drywall cover or brown paper. Any bubbled or lifted edges or areas of drywall cover or brown paper should be cut with a utility knife, and then removed. Apply another coat of oil-based primer/sealer over the entire repair. If the second coat of oil-based primer/sealer has successfully held the cover and brown paper layers intact, then go to *Step 5*. If the repair area continues to bubble or lift, then consider covering the area with an aluminum-reinforced wall repair patch *(See Page 115)*, or have the damaged area of drywall replaced.

    Oil-based quick-drying primer/sealer will almost always hold damaged drywall cover edges and brown paper layers together after the loose, bubbled and lifted areas are removed. I have seen this repair technique fail only one time in over twenty years. In that situation, the drywall was severely damaged after wallpaper removal and sections of drywall had to be replaced.

2. Apply a second coat of oil-based primer/sealer after *Step 4* in cases of severe drywall cover or brown paper damage. The second coat of oil-based primer/sealer provides additional sealing ability to both hold damaged areas together, and to prevent the moisture from drywall joint compound or applied paint from causing further damage. The application of a second coat of oil-based primer/sealer helps to better your odds of successfully completing this repair over severely damaged areas of the drywall cover.

Repairing Surface Defects

Surface defects are problem areas on ceiling and wall surfaces that are often the result of substandard surface preparation or repair work. Older surfaces may have a collection of surface defects that date back to previous painting jobs. Newer surfaces may have a few defects after construction or remodeling. Regardless of their age, some surface defects can worsen over time; and all surface defects detract from the overall appearance of the painted finish.

Repair all surface defects before the application of paint, decorative paint, faux finish, mural art and stencils. Avoid the temptation to just "paint them over." Even minor surface defects will still be visible after the application of paint, and gloss-finished paints will often accentuate surface defects. The surface defects covered in this chapter are listed in *Table 7.1, on the next page.*

Topics covered in Chapter 7 Surface defects	Page
1. Surface grit	162
2. Air bubble holes in applied drywall joint compound	164
3. Inadequate drywall joint compound application over drywall joint tape	166
4. Lifting or bubbling of drywall joint tape	168
5. Inadequate sanding of drywall joint compound	171
6. Inadequate wet sanding of drywall joint compound	173
7. Raised drywall cover damage caused by sanding	176
8. Protruding drywall screw heads	178

Table 7.1

CHAPTER 7 OBJECTIVE

The ability to recognize and repair any of the surface defects covered in this chapter.

Figure 7.1
Surface grit.

SURFACE GRIT

Surface grit consists of small particles of dirt or dried material that have become part of the painted surface. These particles may have been in the paint during application. They may also have been blown onto the surface from the floor or a drop cloth during paint spraying. Grit blown onto the surface during paint spraying is often found near the bottom of walls. *(Fig. 7.1)*

Tools and materials

Eye and respiratory system protection, 6" taping knife, putty knife, fine/medium-grit sanding sponge, wiping cloth or towel, oil-based quick-drying primer/sealer, empty paint can, "all paints" paintbrush, 9" roller frame with ³/₈" nap cover and extension rolling pole, rolling pan, paint thinner and hand cleaner.

Steps

1. Wear eye and respiratory system protection.
   (See Pages 19-20 for eye and respiratory system protection information)

2. Remove surface grit with a putty knife or scraper. Sand the repair surface with the medium-grit side of a sanding sponge. Finish sanding with the fine-grit side.

3. Remove sanding dust with a wiping cloth or towel. Slightly dampening the wiping cloth or towel will help to control dust. Allow any surface moisture to dry before going to *the next step*. If sanding has left the surface smooth, then go to *Step 7*.

4. Using a 6" taping knife, apply joint compound to flush-fill surface indentations resulting from grit removal. Skim coat groups of surface indentations. Allow drying. Apply a second coat of joint compound, if needed. Allow drying.
   (See Using The 6" Taping Knife For Flush-Fills, starting on Page 60)
   (See Skim coating, starting on Page 76)

5. Sand dried joint compound with the fine-grit side of a sanding sponge.

6. Remove sanding dust with a wiping cloth or towel. Slightly dampening the wiping cloth or towel will help to control dust. Allow any surface moisture to dry before going to *Step 7*.

7. Stir then pour oil-based quick-drying primer/sealer into an empty paint can. Two or three inches in the paint can will usually be enough to complete the cutting in of one ceiling or wall surface where surface repairs have been completed. Apply a coat of oil-based quick-drying primer/sealer over the repaired surface using a 9" roller frame, ³/₈" nap roller cover and extension rolling pole. A slim roller frame and cover can be used to apply primer/sealer over smaller repairs. Allow drying.

    Note: If oil-based products are no longer available in your area, use a high-quality latex primer/sealer in this step. Follow directions for cleaning tools, hands and skin. Wear any recommended respiratory system protection.

    Note: If other preparation or repair work will be done, then apply primer/sealer in this room or part of the project after all preparation and repair work has been completed.

8. Lightly sand the dried primer/sealer with the fine-grit side of a sanding sponge. Large surfaces can be sanded using a pole sander with 100-grit or 120-grit pole sander paper.

9. Remove sanding dust with a wiping cloth or towel. Slightly dampening the wiping cloth or towel will help to control dust. Allow any surface moisture to dry before going to *Step 10*.

10. Apply paint, decorative paint, faux finish or stencil.

Refer to Chapter 1 for information regarding safety and avoiding spontaneous combustion fire when using paint thinner, turpentine, mineral spirits, denatured alcohol, paint deglosser, oil-based primers and primer/sealers and White-Pigmented Shellac.

Tips and Troubleshooting

Surface grit

In new construction and remodeling, surface grit can often be prevented by vacuuming floors before paint is sprayed.

Air Bubble Holes in Applied Drywall Joint Compound

A thick application of joint compound often causes air bubble holes to form during drying. These holes vary in size, but are approximately the size of the tip of a ballpoint pen, or larger. Air bubble holes in drying joint compound usually form in clusters. Neither primer nor paint can adequately fill these holes and conceal them from view.

Tools and materials

Eye and respiratory system protection, putty knife, 6" taping knife, mud tray with joint compound, fine/medium-grit sanding sponge, pole sander with 100-grit pole sanding paper, wiping cloth or towel, "all paints" paintbrush, 9" rolling frame, 3/8" nap roller cover, rolling pole, rolling pan, oil-based primer/sealer, empty paint can, paint thinner and hand cleaner.

Steps

1. Wear eye and respiratory system protection.
   (See Pages 19-20 for eye and respiratory system protection information)

2. Lightly sand the surface with the fine-grit side of a sanding sponge.

3. Remove sanding dust with a wiping cloth or towel. Slightly dampening the wiping cloth or towel will help to control dust. Allow any surface moisture to dry before going to *Step 4*.

4. Using a 6" taping knife, apply a coat of joint compound to flush-fill air bubble holes. Allow drying. Apply a second coat of joint compound, if needed. Allow drying.

5. Lightly sand dried joint compound with the fine-grit side of a sanding sponge.

6. Remove sanding dust with a wiping cloth or towel. Slightly dampening the wiping cloth or towel will help to control dust. Allow any surface moisture to dry before going to *Step 7*.

7. Stir then pour oil-based quick-drying primer/sealer into an empty paint can. Two or three inches in the paint can will usually be enough to complete the cutting in of one ceiling or wall surface where repairs have been completed. Apply a coat of oil-based quick-drying primer/sealer over the repaired surface using a 9" roller frame, 3/8" nap roller cover and extension rolling pole. A slim roller frame and cover can be used to apply primer/sealer over small repairs. Allow drying.

   Note: If oil-based products are no longer available in your area, use a high-quality latex primer/sealer in this step. Follow directions for cleaning tools, hands and skin. Wear any recommended respiratory system protection.

   Note: If other preparation or repair work will be done, then apply primer/sealer in this room or part of the project after all preparation and repair work has been completed.

8. Lightly sand the dried primer/sealer with the fine-grit side of a sanding sponge. Large surfaces can be sanded using a pole sander with 100-grit or 120-grit pole sander paper.

9. Remove sanding dust with a wiping cloth or towel. Slightly dampening the wiping cloth or towel will help to control dust. Allow any surface moisture to dry before going to *Step 10*.

10. Apply paint, decorative paint, faux finish or stencil.

Refer to Chapter 1 for information regarding safety and avoiding spontaneous combustion fire when using paint thinner, turpentine, mineral spirits, denatured alcohol, paint deglosser, oil-based primers and primer/sealers and White-Pigmented Shellac.

TIPS AND TROUBLESHOOTING

Air bubble holes in applied drywall joint compound

Apply drywall joint compound in thin, even coats to avoid air bubble holes.

Inadequate drywall joint compound application over drywall joint tape

Drywall joint tape must be fully covered with applied drywall joint compound to form a durable joint or inside corner. If any part of the drywall joint tape is visible, then it was not adequately covered with drywall joint compound. An inadequate application of joint compound over drywall joint tape will leave part, or all, of the outline of the tape visible. The mesh pattern of self-adhesive mesh drywall joint tape will be visible if not fully covered with joint compound. Inadequately covered drywall joint tape may not bond durably with the surface, and detracts from the aesthetic value of the painted finish.

Tools and materials

Eye and respiratory system protection, putty knife, 6" taping knife, mud tray with joint compound, fine/medium-grit sanding sponge, pole sander with 100-grit pole sanding paper, wiping cloth or towel, "all paints" paintbrush, 9" rolling frame, ³⁄₈ " nap roller cover, rolling pole, rolling pan, oil-based primer/sealer, empty paint can, paint thinner and hand cleaner.

Steps

1. Wear eye and respiratory system protection.
   (See Pages 19-20 for eye and respiratory system protection information)

2. Visually check the joint tape for lifting and bubbling. Then tap the tape and listen for a hollow sound. If the tape has lifted, bubbled or has an area that sounds hollow, then the tape must be removed: *Go to the next repair method:* Lifting or bubbling of drywall joint tape.

   If the drywall joint tape is solidly in place, then go to *Step 3*.

3. Lightly sand the surface with the fine-grit side of a sanding sponge.

4. Remove sanding dust with a wiping cloth or towel. Slightly dampening the wiping cloth or towel will help to control dust. Allow any surface moisture to dry before going to *Step 5*.

5. Using a 6" taping knife, apply a coat of joint compound to cover the tape. Extend the application an inch or two past the previously applied joint compound. For corner repairs, apply joint compound straight out from the corner two or three inches on each side. Use the taping knife blade to contour the application at the edges, where the application should be its thinnest. Allow drying.

6. Apply a second coat of joint compound using the same technique as in *Step 5*. Corner applications should be extended an inch past the application in *Step 5*. Allow drying.

7. Apply a third coat of joint compound, if needed. Extend the application an inch past the last application to conceal the repair. A partial application may be sufficient. Allow drying. Repeat this step, if necessary.

8. Use the fine-grit side of a sanding sponge to sand the repair. Remove sanding dust with a wiping cloth or towel. Slightly dampening the wiping cloth or towel will help to control dust. Allow any surface moisture to dry before going to *Step 9*.

Any exposed tape should be covered with joint compound. Allow drying and then repeat *Step 8*.

9. Stir then pour oil-based quick-drying primer/sealer into an empty paint can. Two or three inches in the paint can will usually be enough to complete the cutting in of one ceiling or wall surface where repairs have been completed. Apply a coat of oil-based quick-drying primer/sealer over the repaired surface using a 9" roller frame, 3/8" nap roller cover and extension rolling pole. A slim roller frame and cover can be used to apply primer/sealer over small repairs. Allow drying.

   Note: If oil-based products are no longer available in your area, use a high-quality latex primer/sealer in this step. Follow directions for cleaning tools, hands and skin. Wear any recommended respiratory system protection.

   Note: If other preparation or repair work will be done, then apply primer/sealer in this room or part of the project after all preparation and repair work has been completed.

10. Lightly sand the dried primer/sealer with the fine-grit side of a sanding sponge. Large surfaces can be sanded using a pole sander with 100-grit or 120-grit pole sander paper.

11. Remove sanding dust with a wiping cloth or towel. Slightly dampening the wiping cloth or towel will help to control dust. Allow any surface moisture to dry before going to *Step 12*.

12. Apply paint, decorative paint, faux finish or stencil.

Refer to Chapter 1 for information regarding safety and avoiding spontaneous combustion fire when using paint thinner, turpentine, mineral spirits, denatured alcohol, paint deglosser, oil-based primers and primer/sealers and White-Pigmented Shellac.

Tips and Troubleshooting

Inadequate drywall joint compound application over drywall joint tape

1. Cover drywall joint tape completely with drywall joint compound. Exposed areas of the joint tape will be visible after painting.

2. Three coats of drywall joint compound may be needed to adequately cover some areas of exposed drywall joint tape.

3. Partial, or spot, coats of drywall joint compound may be enough to cover some areas.

4. Apply joint compound in thin, even coats to avoid air bubble holes.

LIFTING OR BUBBLING OF DRYWALL JOINT TAPE

Paper drywall joint tape may lift or bubble (also called "blistering") from the surface if not properly installed. Lifting of drywall joint tape occurs when ends or edges become loose. A joint tape bubble appears as a bulge or rounded protrusion extending out from the surface. Joint tape that has either lifted or bubbled is no longer adhered to surface and must be replaced.

Tools and materials

Eye and respiratory system protection, putty knife, scraper, 6" taping knife, mud tray with joint compound, self-adhesive mesh drywall joint tape, scissors, utility knife, fine/medium-grit sanding sponge, pole sander with 100-grit pole sanding paper, wiping cloth or towel, "all paints" paintbrush, 9" rolling frame, 3/8" nap roller cover, rolling pole, rolling pan, empty paint can, oil-based primer/sealer, paint thinner and hand cleaner.

Steps

1. Wear eye and respiratory system protection.
   (See Pages 19-20 for eye and respiratory system protection information)

2. Using a putty knife or scraper, remove all drywall joint tape that has lifted, bubbled or become loose. A utility knife can be used to carefully cut sections of tape before removal.

3. Lightly sand the surface with the fine-grit side of a sanding sponge.

4. Remove sanding dust with a wiping cloth or towel. Slightly dampening the wiping cloth or towel will help to control dust. Allow any surface moisture to dry before going to *Step 5*.

5. Replace removed drywall joint tape with self-adhesive mesh drywall joint tape. *(See self-adhesive mesh drywall joint tape, on Page 143)*

6. Using a 6" taping knife, apply a coat of joint compound to cover the tape. Extend the application an inch or two past the previously applied joint compound. The mesh should be filled but the tape should still visible after the first coat. Remove excess. Allow drying.

7. Apply a second coat of joint compound extending an inch or two past the previously applied joint compound.

   For corner repairs, apply joint compound two or three inches out from each side of the corner. Use the taping knife blade to contour the application. The application should be thinnest at the edges. Allow drying.

8. Apply a third coat of joint compound, if needed. Extend the application an inch past the last application. A partial application may be sufficient to conceal the repair. Allow drying. Repeat this step, if necessary.

9. Use the fine-grit side of a sanding sponge to sand the repair.

10. Remove sanding dust with a wiping cloth or towel. Slightly dampening the wiping cloth or towel will help to control dust. Allow any surface moisture to dry before going to *Step 11*.

    Any exposed tape should be covered with joint compound. Allow drying and then repeat *Step 9*.

11. Stir then pour oil-based quick-drying primer/sealer into an empty paint can. Two or three inches in the paint can will usually be enough to complete the cutting in of one ceiling or wall surface where drywall joint tape repairs have been completed. Apply a coat of oil-based quick-drying primer/sealer over the repaired surface using a 9" roller frame, 3/8" nap roller cover and extension rolling pole. A slim roller frame and cover can be used to apply primer/sealer over small repairs. Allow drying.

    Note: If oil-based products are no longer available in your area, use a high-quality latex primer/sealer in this step. Follow directions for cleaning tools, hands and skin. Wear any recommended respiratory system protection.

    Note: If other preparation or repair work will be done, then apply primer/sealer in this room or part of the project after all preparation and repair work has been completed.

12. Lightly sand the dried primer/sealer with the fine-grit side of a sanding sponge. Large surfaces can be sanded using a pole sander with 100-grit or 120-grit pole sander paper.

13. Remove sanding dust with a wiping cloth or towel. Slightly dampening the wiping cloth or towel will help to control dust. Allow any surface moisture to dry before going to *Step 14*.

14. Apply paint, decorative paint, faux finish or stencil.

Refer to Chapter 1 for information regarding safety and avoiding spontaneous combustion fire when using paint thinner, turpentine, mineral spirits, denatured alcohol, paint deglosser, oil-based primers and primer/sealers and White-Pigmented Shellac.

Tips and Troubleshooting

Lifting or bubbling of drywall joint tape

Removal of drywall joint tape often leaves a recessed area on the surface. This recessed area is bordered with the drywall joint compound that was originally used to cover the joint tape. After replacing the tape, a deep recess will require two or three coats of joint compound to restore the recessed area back to the contour of the original drywall finishing job. Apply joint compound over the recessed area, and then allow drying. Repeat until the recessed area is built back to the level of the surrounding surface. After the recessed area has been restored, apply full coats of joint compound to correctly shape and contour the repair.

Inadequate sanding of drywall joint compound

Inadequate sanding of finished drywall often results in areas of joint compound that are not smooth or uniform. The application of primer/sealer or paint will not conceal the defects left when joint compound is not adequately sanded. The higher the gloss of your painted finish, the more noticeable inadequately-sanded surfaces become. If primer or paint has already been applied over inadequately sanded joint compound, use the skim coating technique to make the surface look smooth and uniform.

Tools and materials

Eye and respiratory system protection, putty knife, 6" taping knife, mud tray with joint compound, fine/medium-grit sanding sponge, pole sander with 100-grit pole sanding paper, wiping cloth or towel, "all paints" paintbrush, 9" rolling frame, 3/8" nap roller cover, rolling pole, rolling pan, oil-based primer/sealer, empty paint can, paint thinner and hand cleaner.

Steps

1. Wear eye and respiratory system protection.
   (*See Pages 19-20 for eye and respiratory system protection information*)

2. Use the fine-grit side of a sanding sponge to sand any areas of unsanded, or poorly-sanded, joint compound. The medium-grit side can be used when beginning to sand edges and areas of heavy joint compound application. For areas sanded with medium-grit, follow by finish sanding with the fine-grit side of the sanding sponge.

3. Remove sanding dust with a wiping cloth or towel. Slightly dampening the wiping cloth or towel will help to control dust. Allow any surface moisture to dry before going to *Step 4*.

   Apply joint compound to cover any exposed drywall joint tape. Also apply joint compound, if needed, to properly shape and contour the repair. Partial, or spot, coats of joint compound may be sufficient. Allow drying, and then sand with the fine-grit side of a sanding sponge. Remove sanding dust with a wiping cloth or towel.

4. Stir then pour oil-based quick-drying primer/sealer into an empty paint can. Two or three inches in the paint can will usually be enough to complete the cutting in of one ceiling or wall surface where repairs have been completed. Apply a coat of oil-based quick-drying primer/sealer over the repaired surface using a 9" roller frame, 3/8" nap roller cover and extension rolling pole. A slim roller frame and cover can be used to apply primer/sealer over small repairs. Allow drying.

   Note: If oil-based products are no longer available in your area, use a high-quality latex primer/sealer in this step. Follow directions for cleaning tools, hands and skin. Wear any recommended respiratory system protection.

   Note: If other preparation or repair work will be done, then apply primer/sealer in this room or part of the project after all preparation and repair work has been completed.

5. Lightly sand the dried primer/sealer with the fine-grit side of a sanding sponge. Large surfaces can be sanded using a pole sander with 100-grit or 120-grit pole sander paper.

6. Remove sanding dust with a wiping cloth or towel. Slightly dampening the wiping cloth or towel will help to control dust. Allow any surface moisture to dry before going to *Step 7*.

7. Apply paint, decorative paint, faux finish or stencil.

Refer to Chapter 1 for information regarding safety and avoiding spontaneous combustion fire when using paint thinner, turpentine, mineral spirits, denatured alcohol, paint deglosser, oil-based primers and primer/sealers and White-Pigmented Shellac.

TIPS AND TROUBLESHOOTING

Incomplete sanding of drywall joint compound

Inspect repaired surfaces after dried primer/sealer has been sanded and wiped clean. *(Step 6)* Apply joint compound, if needed, to fill surface defects and to complete the correct shape and contour of repairs. If additional joint compound application is needed, begin with *Step 2* after the applied joint compound has dried. Spot prime any areas that needed additional joint compound.

Note: Spot priming areas that needed additional joint compound is acceptable in this situation when the primer/sealer used in *Step 4* **is the same as the primer/sealer used for spot priming.**

When the spot coat primer and base-coat primer are the same product, then a uniform substrate is maintained.

Inadequate Wet Sanding of Drywall Joint Compound

In an effort to eliminate joint compound sanding dust, new construction drywall surfaces are often wet-sanded. During wet sanding, damp cloths or sponges are used instead of pole sanders, sanding sponges and sandpaper. Wet sanding eliminates much of the sanding dust, but does not always provide a smooth, uniform surface for priming and painting. When dry, previously wet-sanded joint compound can be difficult to sand precisely.

Why wet-sanded joint compound can be difficult to sand

Wetting dried joint compound can cause the joint compound to swell and become grainy. The borders, or edges, of wet-sanded joint compound often appear puffy and swollen; and wet-sanded joint compound may not gradually contour, or "feather," when sanded. Faced with this situation, additional coats of joint compound should be applied two or three inches past the areas of affected wet-sanded joint compound. When dry, the new application should sand precisely.

Tools and materials

Eye and respiratory system protection, putty knife, 6" taping knife, mud tray with joint compound, fine/medium-grit sanding sponge, pole sander with 100-grit pole sanding paper, wiping cloth or towel, "all paints" paintbrush, 9" rolling frame, 3/8" nap roller cover, rolling pole, rolling pan, oil-based primer/sealer, empty paint can, paint thinner and hand cleaner.

Steps

1. Wear eye and respiratory system protection.
   (*See Pages 19-20 for eye and respiratory system protection information*)

2. Use the medium-grit side of a sanding sponge to sand areas of joint compound that are not smooth or uniform. Finish sand with the fine-grit side of a sanding sponge. The goal of this step is to reduce "high" areas and edges. Skim coating in *Step 4* will make these areas uniform.

3. Remove sanding dust with a wiping cloth or towel. Slightly dampening the wiping cloth or towel will help to control dust. Allow any surface moisture to dry before going to *Step 4*.

4. Skim coat any area of joint compound that is not smooth or uniform. Two or three skim coats may be needed. Joint compound should be applied two or three inches past the edges of wet-sanding defects. In some situations, it may be necessary to skim coat over most, or all, wet-sanded joint compound.

5. Apply a second coat of joint compound. Allow drying. Apply a third coat, if needed. Allow drying.

6. Use the fine-grit side of a sanding sponge to sand all joint compounded areas, both wet-sanded and skim coated.

7. Remove sanding dust with a wiping cloth or towel. Slightly dampening the wiping cloth or towel will help to control dust. Allow any surface moisture to dry before going to *Step 8*.

8. Stir then pour oil-based quick-drying primer/sealer into an empty paint can. Two or three inches in the paint can will usually be enough to complete the cutting in of one ceiling or wall surface where repairs have been completed. Apply a coat of oil-based quick-drying primer/sealer over the repaired surface using a 9" roller frame, ³/₈" nap roller cover and extension rolling pole. A slim roller frame and cover can be used to apply primer/sealer over small repairs. Allow drying.

   Note: If oil-based products are no longer available in your area, use a high-quality latex primer/sealer in this step. Follow directions for cleaning tools, hands and skin. Wear any recommended respiratory system protection.

   Note: If other preparation or repair work will be done, then apply primer/sealer in this room or part of the project after all preparation and repair work has been completed.

9. Lightly sand the dried primer/sealer with the fine-grit side of a sanding sponge. Large surfaces can be sanded using a pole sander with 100-grit or 120-grit pole sander paper.

10. Remove sanding dust with a wiping cloth or towel. Slightly dampening the wiping cloth or towel will help to control dust. Allow any surface moisture to dry before going to *Step 11*.

11. Inspect surfaces, and then apply joint compound, if needed. Repeat *Steps 6-11* if additional joint compound is applied.

12. Apply paint, decorative paint, faux finish or stencil.

Refer to Chapter 1 for information regarding safety and avoiding spontaneous combustion fire when using paint thinner, turpentine, mineral spirits, denatured alcohol, paint deglosser, oil-based primers and primer/sealers and White-Pigmented Shellac.

Chapter 7 Repairing Surface Defects

TIPS AND TROUBLESHOOTING

Wet-sanded drywall joint compound

1. For best results in new construction surface preparation, avoid wet sanding unless dust sensitivity is a health concern.

2. Inspect repaired surfaces after primer/sealer has been sanded, and sanding dust has been removed. *(Step 11)* Inspect surfaces in varying lights to see if any areas need additional joint compound application. Large repair areas will often need spot fills, or partial coats, to achieve a uniform appearance.

Estimated Time to Complete These Techniques

The estimated time to complete the repair of a new construction drywall surface defect is thirty minutes. The size of the area and the condition of the surface will determine the time needed.

Note: Estimated time to complete steps includes drying times for repair compounds and primer/sealer. Refer to the directions on the container for drying times of repair compounds and primer/sealer. Humid conditions will lengthen drying times. Other preparation and repair work can be done in the room while waiting for repair compounds to dry.

RAISED DRYWALL COVER DAMAGE CAUSED BY SANDING

Sanding joint compound on new drywall can cause areas of the drywall cover near sanded areas to appear fuzzy. The fuzzy-looking areas are fibers of the drywall cover that have been raised during sanding. These fibers often become stubbly after the application of primer/sealer and paint. This problem is common, and not a cause for concern. If excessive sanding has resulted in the drywall cover being worn through to the brown paper layers beneath, then refer to the section: REPAIRING DRYWALL COVER DAMAGE, on Page 152.

Tools and materials

Eye and respiratory system protection, putty knife, 6" taping knife, mud tray with joint compound, fine/medium-grit sanding sponge, pole sander with 100-grit pole sanding paper, wiping cloth or towel, oil-based quick-drying primer/sealer, "all paints" paintbrush, 9" rolling frame, 3/8" nap roller cover, rolling pole, rolling pan, oil-based primer/sealer, empty paint can, paint thinner and hand cleaner.

Steps

1. Wear eye protection and respiratory system protection.
   (*See Pages 19-20 for eye and respiratory system protection information*)

2. If the drywall has already been primed or painted, then sand affected areas using the fine-grit side of a sanding sponge. Sand difficult areas with the medium-grit side, and then finish sand with the fine-grit side.

   On bare drywall, apply one coat of oil-based quick-drying primer/sealer over areas where fibers have been raised. Allow drying. Sand the repair surface using the fine-grit side of a sanding sponge. Sand difficult areas with the medium-grit side, and then finish sand with the fine-grit side.

3. Remove sanding dust with a wiping cloth or towel. Slightly dampening the wiping cloth or towel will help to control dust. Allow any surface moisture to dry before going to *Step 4*.

4. If the surface is smooth after sanding, then go to *Step 5*.

   If the surface is rough, then skim coat areas of roughness with joint compound. Allow drying. Apply a second coat of joint compound, if needed. Allow drying.

   Sand dried joint compound with the fine-grit side of a sanding sponge. Remove sanding dust with a wiping cloth or towel. Slightly dampening the wiping cloth or towel will help to control dust. Allow any surface moisture to dry before going to *Step 5*.

5. Stir then pour oil-based quick-drying primer/sealer into an empty paint can. Two or three inches in the paint can will usually be enough to complete the cutting in of one ceiling or wall surface where repairs have been completed. Apply a coat of oil-based quick-drying primer/sealer over the repaired surface using a 9" roller frame, 3/8" nap roller cover and extension rolling pole. A slim roller frame and cover can be used to apply primer/sealer over small repairs. Allow drying.

   Note: If oil-based products are no longer available in your area, use a high-quality latex primer/sealer in this step. Follow directions for cleaning tools, hands and skin. Wear any recommended respiratory system protection.

Note: If other preparation or repair work will be done, then apply primer/sealer in this room or part of the project after all preparation and repair work has been completed.

6. Lightly sand the dried primer/sealer with the fine-grit side of a sanding sponge. Large surfaces can be sanded using a pole sander with 100-grit pole sander paper.

7. Remove sanding dust with a wiping cloth or towel. Slightly dampening the wiping cloth or towel will help to control dust. Allow any surface moisture to dry before going to *Step 8*.

8. Apply paint, decorative paint, faux finish or stencil.

Refer to Chapter 1 for information regarding safety and avoiding spontaneous combustion fire when using paint thinner, turpentine, mineral spirits, denatured alcohol, paint deglosser, oil-based primers and primer/sealers and White-Pigmented Shellac.

TIPS AND TROUBLESHOOTING

Raised drywall cover damage caused by sanding

1. When sanding new drywall, use light, careful sanding strokes on the edges of applied drywall joint compound. Forceful sanding strokes on the edges of applied joint compound can raise the fibers of the cover, and cause cover tearing.

2. The drywall cover itself does not need to be sanded.

3. Oil-based quick-drying primer/sealer is best for coating and hardening raised drywall cover fibers before sanding. Its hard finish enables smooth sanding of most raised drywall cover fibers.

   If oil-based products are no longer available in your area, ask your paint dealer to recommend another product specifically for this repair.

Protruding drywall screw heads

New construction drywall is now almost always fastened with drywall screws. The screws are driven just below the surface and covered with joint compound. After sanding, the area above the drywall screw is flush to the surface. If drywall screws are not driven below the surface, a small bump or protrusion will often be visible.

Tools and materials

Eye and respiratory system protection, 6" taping knife, putty knife, mud tray with joint compound, fine/medium-grit sanding sponge or 80-grit sandpaper, drill driver with magnetic drive guide, hammer, drywall screws, wiping cloth or towel, "all paints" paintbrush, 9" rolling frame, 3/8" nap roller cover, rolling pole, rolling pan, oil-based primer/sealer, empty paint can, paint thinner and hand cleaner.

Steps

1. Wear eye and respiratory system protection.
   (*See Pages 19-20 for eye and respiratory system protection information*)

2. If the screw head has caused only a minor surface protrusion, then joint compound can be applied to blend the protrusion into the surrounding surface.

   If the screw head has caused a large protrusion, then remove the material over the screw and try to drive it just below the surface with a drill driver and magnetic drive guide. If successful, cover the driven screw with joint compound until flush to the surface.

   Should you be unable to drive the screw below the surface, then try to back it out and replace it with a smaller screw. If successful, cover the driven screw with joint compound until flush to the surface.

   If the screw cannot be driven just below the surface, or backed out from the surface, then apply joint compound with a round shape and proper contour to help conceal the protrusion.

3. Sand the repair area with the fine-grit side of a sanding sponge.

4. Remove sanding dust with a wiping cloth or towel. Slightly dampening the wiping cloth or towel will help to control dust. Allow any surface moisture to dry before going to *Step 5*.

   Apply additional joint compound, if needed. Allow drying, and then repeat *Step 3*.

5. Stir then pour oil-based quick-drying primer/sealer into an empty paint can. Two or three inches in the paint can will usually be enough to complete the cutting in of one ceiling or wall surface where repairs have been completed. Apply a coat of oil-based quick-drying primer/sealer over the repaired surface using a 9" roller frame, 3/8" nap roller cover and extension rolling pole. A slim roller frame and cover can be used to apply primer/sealer over small repairs. Allow drying.

   Note: If oil-based products are no longer available in your area, use a high-quality latex primer/sealer in this step. Follow directions for cleaning tools, hands and skin. Wear any recommended respiratory system protection.

Note: If other preparation or repair work will be done, then apply primer/sealer in this room or part of the project after all preparation and repair work has been completed.

6. Lightly sand the dried primer/sealer with the fine-grit side of a sanding sponge. Large surfaces can be sanded using a pole sander with 100-grit pole sander paper.

7. Remove sanding dust with a wiping cloth or towel. Slightly dampening the wiping cloth or towel will help to control dust. Allow any surface moisture to dry before going to *Step 8*.

8. Apply paint, decorative paint, faux finish or stencil.

Refer to Chapter 1 for information regarding safety and avoiding spontaneous combustion fire when using paint thinner, turpentine, mineral spirits, denatured alcohol, paint deglosser, oil-based primers and primer/sealers and White-Pigmented Shellac.

TIPS AND TROUBLESHOOTING

Protruding drywall screw heads

A 1¼" drywall screw will often work well as a replacement screw when a 1³/₈" screw is removed.

This book is dedicated to the memory
of my mentor and friend,

Ralph W. "Bill" Cummins

SECTION III

Appendices and Index

Appendices

Appendix 1

REFERENCE OF SURFACE PREPARATION TECHNIQUES AND REPAIRS — PAGE

Chapter 3

Cleaning wallpaper and border paste residue	49

Chapter 5

Application of drywall joint compound	64
Application of lightweight spackling compound	68
Application of spackling compound	72
Skim coating ceiling and wall surfaces with drywall joint compound	77
Skim coating wood trim surfaces with spackling compound	82
Using painter's putty to fill nail sets and miter gaps on wood surfaces	85
Sanding	88
Caulking	95
Priming and sealing	100

Chapter 6

Repairing holes and damaged areas with a wall repair patch	115
Repairing holes and indentations in wood surfaces with wood filler	120
Repairing drywall nail pops	124
Repair of surfaces with plastic anchors and metal Molly bolt jackets	131
Supporting cracked ceiling drywall and refastening sagging ceiling drywall	134
Repairing cracks with self-adhesive mesh drywall joint tape and joint compound	144
Repairing drywall cover damage	152

Chapter 7

Surface grit	162
Air bubble holes in applied drywall joint compound	164
Inadequate drywall joint compound application over drywall joint tape	166
Lifting or bubbling of drywall joint tape	168
Inadequate sanding of drywall joint compound	171
Inadequate wet-sanding of drywall joint compound	173
Raised drywall cover damage caused by sanding	176
Protruding drywall screw heads	178

Appendix 2

REFERENCE OF SURFACE PREP TIP BOXES   PAGE

Chapter 1

Two-Drop Rule	22

Chapter 2

Stirring primers and paints	31
Disposing of primers, paints, materials and supplies	31
Cover furniture with two sheets of plastic	32

Chapter 3

When to consult with a professional	38
Getting the job right the first time	39
Removing adhesive residue from clear tapes, masking tapes and stickers	45

Chapter 5

Applying repair compounds	67
Preparing ahead	71
Check your work at different times of the day in both natural and artificial light	71
Remove flecks before sanding	89
Use worn sanding tools for extra-smooth surface sanding	89
Removing multiple layers of paint from wood surfaces	93
Primer and sealer technology	104
Do not skimp on priming and sealing	105

Chapter 6

Avoid applying excessive amounts of drywall joint compound when crafting surface preparation repairs	128
Careful sanding of completed repairs	130

Index

A

Adhesive remover 45

Ammonia 45

Anchor repair (plastic) 108-109, 131-133, 184

Asbestos 18

B

Bleach 45

Blowtorch 93

C

Cat's Paw tool 129

Caulk, Caulking 18, 22, 30, 34, 58-59, 95-99

    Adhesive caulk 30, 95-96

    Caulk gun 30, 36, 96-97

Chemical paint deglosser (See Paint deglosser)

Children (protecting during surface preparation) 23, 88

Cleaning 17, 20-21, 34-35, 40, 45-46, 49, 101

    Soiled surfaces 40, 45, 101

    Mildewed surfaces 46

    Wallpaper and border paste residue 40, 45, 49, 101

Crack repair 28, 108-110, 134, 140-151

Cummins, Bill 181

D

Denatured alcohol 20, 24, 34-35

Disposal of primers, paints, materials and supplies 31

Index

Drill driver 125, 135, 137, 178

Drywall 11, 28-29, 40, 42, 44, 46-47, 64, 68, 72, 76, 101-103, 108-109, 115, 119, 124-126, 131, 133-142, 146-147, 152-156, 160, 164-173, 175-179

    Repair of torn cover 152-156

    Repair of sanding damage 176-177

    Nails 109, 124, 127, 129, 134-135, 137, 139

        Nail dimple, dimpling 125-126, 129, 131, 134, 137

        Nail pop 108, 126

            Repair 124-127

    Priming 102-103

    Screws 109, 124-125, 134-135, 137, 139, 160, 178

Drywall joint compound 18, 28, 30, 58, 60-67, 76-78, 80-81, 90-91, 102-103, 107-114, 119, 124-126, 128-130, 133-134, 140-142, 144-152, 154, 156, 160, 164-167, 170-173, 175, 177

    Application 64-66

    Air bubble holes in dried joint compound 66, 160, 164-165, 167

    Inadequate application over drywall joint tape 166-167

    Inadequate sanding 171-172

    Inadequate wet-sanding 173-175

Drywall joint tape 28, 107-108, 113-114, 140-152, 154-155, 160, 166-171

    Paper 28, 143, 145, 168

        Lifting and bubbling (blistering) 28, 160, 166, 168-170

    Self-adhesive mesh 28, 107-108, 114, 140, 143-152, 154-155, 166, 184

Duster 68, 145

E

Ear and hearing protection 21

Electric sander 88

EPA's Renovate, Repair and Painting Rule (RRP) 9, 16, 88

Extension cord (heavy gauge) 25, 52

Eye protection 19-20, 88, 93

F

Feathering 94, 105, 110, 173

    Sanded edges 94, 110, 173

    Brushed material 105

Fleck 89-90, 94, 103, 114

Flush-fills 58-63, 66, 72-73, 75, 82, 87-91, 93, 107, 123, 129-133, 162, 164

G

H

Hammer 11, 72, 124-126, 129, 131-133, 135, 137

    Drywall hammer 125-126, 129, 135, 137

Hand cleaner 34

Hand protection 19, 21, 35, 93

Heat gun 93

HEPA attachment for sander 88

HEPA vacuum 88

I

J

Joint compound *(See Drywall joint compound)*

K

Index

L

Lead, lead-based paint 9, 16-17, 88, 91-92

Lightweight spackling compound 29-30, 58, 63, 67-70, 89, 131-132, 184

      Application 68-70

Lubricant 34

M

Mildew 40, 43, 46, 76, 115, 119

Mineral spirits 20, 24, 35

Mold 17, 40, 43, 47, 76, 115, 119

Molly bolt jacket repair 108-109, 131-133, 184

N

Nail pop, Nail pop repair *(See Drywall nail pop)*

Nail sets, Nail set tool reference 29, 58-59, 85-87, 132, 184

      Holes to fill with Painter's Putty 29, 58-59, 85-87, 184

Non-flush repairs 66, 107-110, 112-114

O

OSHA 20-21

P

Paint remover 93

Paint thinner 24, 35

Painter's putty 29, 58-59, 85-87, 184

Painting masking tapes 33

Pets (protecting during surface preparation) 23

Plaster 28-30, 40, 42, 47-48, 64, 68, 72, 76, 101, 115, 119, 131, 140-141, 147

    Efflorescence 42, 47

    Hawk tool 80

    Inspecting 42, 47

    Priming new and repaired 101

Plastic 32

Pole sander 34, 48, 65, 69, 77-79, 91, 94, 101-103, 113, 126, 133, 138, 145, 150, 163-164, 166-167, 169, 171, 173-174, 177, 179

Priming and sealing 100-105

    Application 105

    After wallpaper and border removal 101

    Bare wood 103

    Barrier coat (between oil-based and latex paint layers) 100

    Before decorative paint, faux finish, mural art and stencils 102

    Joint compound repairs 102

    New drywall 102-103

    Paint bubbles, bubbling (helping to prevent with an oil-based primer/sealer) 103

    Plaster 101

    Spot priming 104-105

    Undercoater or Underbody 30, 35, 86, 100

    Wood with knots 103

Primer/sealer 20, 24, 28-30, 35, 43-44, 47-48, 59, 65, 69, 74, 77, 79, 83, 86, 88, 92, 97, 99-105, 117-118, 121, 126, 131-133, 137-138, 145 148-150, 152-153, 155-156, 163-165, 167, 169, 171-179

    Tinted 105

Putty knife 59-60, 62-64, 67-68, 73, 77-78, 81-82, 85, 89, 116, 120, 125, 140-143, 148, 151, 162, 168

Q

R

Respiratory system protection 19-20, 88, 93

S

Sanding 16, 20-21, 30, 32, 35, 45, 48, 58-60, 62-69, 72-79, 81-83, 85-94, 101-103, 110, 112-118, 120-121, 125-126, 128, 130, 132-133, 137-138, 142-143, 145, 148-150, 152, 154-155, 160, 162-164, 166-169, 171-179, 184-185

    "Dustless" sanding 88, 92, 94

        Wet sanding 92, 173, 175

Sanding sponge 48, 64-65, 68-69, 72-74, 77-79, 82-83, 91, 93-94, 101, 103, 113-118, 120-121, 125-126, 130, 132-133, 137-138, 142, 145, 148-150, 152, 154-155, 162-164, 166-169, 171, 173-174, 176-179

Sandpaper 64, 68-69, 72-76, 79, 81-83, 85, 90-94, 99, 103, 113, 120, 132, 142, 149, 173

    Folding, Folded 72-73, 90, 94, 113

    Latex surface sandpaper 90

Shellac (White-Pigmented) 20, 24, 30, 34, 100, 103-104

Skim coating 11, 28-29, 58-60, 66, 72, 76-84, 110, 171, 173, 176, 184

    Ceiling and wall surfaces 28, 58, 60, 66, 77-81, 171, 173, 176, 184

    Wood surfaces 11, 29, 58, 60, 72, 82-84, 184

Spackling compound 18, 29-30, 43, 58, 60, 63, 67, 72-75, 82-84, 87, 91-92, 102, 120, 123, 184

    Application 72-75

Spontaneous combustion fire (Avoiding) 24, 93

Stencils 9, 44, 47, 57, 59, 90, 101-104, 115

Stirring primers and paints 31

Surface grit 160, 162-163, 184

T

Taping knife 22, 48, 58-64, 66-68, 70, 73, 77-78, 80-82, 109-112, 114, 116-117, 120, 125, 137, 142-145, 148-149, 154, 162, 164, 166, 168, 176, 178

    Tips for use 62-63

Tri-sodium phosphate cleaner (TSP, TSP 90, TSP Substitute) 21, 34, 45

Turpentine 24, 35

Two-Drop Rule 22

U

Underbody or Undercoater primer *(See Priming and Sealing)*

Utility knife 22, 95-96, 142-143, 146, 151-152, 156, 168

V

W

Wall repair patch (Aluminum-reinforced) 30, 107-110, 114-119, 156, 184

Wallpaper paste 21, 34-35, 39, 41, 44, 48, 101, 184

    Remover 34, 48

    Residue removal 48

Wiping cloth 34

Wood filler 18, 29, 43, 60, 87, 91-92, 108-109, 120-123, 184

Work gloves 21, 35, 45-46, 49, 142

    Regular or light-weight work gloves 21, 35, 142

    Chemical-resistant rubber work gloves 21, 35, 45-46, 49

Work lights 23, 51-53, 71

X

Y

Z

The End